MW01223554

Mississauga

BUILDING ON EXCELLENCE

The Mississauga Board of Trade and Community Communications, Inc., would like to express
our gratitude to these companies for their leadership in the development of this book.

We would also like to thank the following companies for their patronage of this project:

C. D. Sonter Management
Lakeview GS
St. Lawrence Cement

Mississauga
BUILDING ON EXCELLENCE

By Stuart Foxman
Corporate Profiles by Bruce O'Neill
Featuring the Photography of Michael Scholz

Photo by *Michael Scholz*

Credits

Mississauga
BUILDING ON EXCELLENCE

By **Stuart Foxman**
Corporate Profiles by **Bruce O'Neill**
Featuring the Photography of **Michael Scholz**

Community Communications, Inc.
Publisher: **Ronald P. Beers**

Staff for *Mississauga: Building on Excellence*

Acquisitions: **Henry Beers**
Publisher's Sales Associate: **Ken Laverty**
Editor in Chief: **Wendi Lewis**
Managing Editor: **Kurt R. Niland**
Profile Editor: **Amanda J. Burbank**
Editorial Assistants: **Krewe Maynard, Eleanor Planer
and Deb Carroll**
Design Director: **Scott Phillips**
Designer: **Ron Ridings**
Photo Editors: **Kurt R. Niland and Ron Ridings**
Production Manager: **Jarrod Stiff**
Pre-Press and Separations: **Artcraft Graphic Productions**
National Sales Manager: **Keely Smith**
Sales Assistants: **Brandon Maddox and Annette Lozier**
Accounting Services: **Stephanie Perez**

Community Communications, Inc.
Montgomery, Alabama

David M. Williamson, Chief Executive Officer
Ronald P. Beers, President
W. David Brown, Chief Operating Officer

© 2001 Community Communications
All Rights Reserved
Published 2001
Printed in Canada
First Edition
ISBN: 1-58192-038-5

Every effort has been made to ensure the accuracy of the information herein.
However, the authors and Community Communications are not responsible for
any errors or omissions that might have occurred.

Table of Contents

Chapter One

FRIENDS AND NEIGHBOURS

Mississauga's success isn't just an accident of geography. It's the product of careful planning and the rich heritage of the numerous towns, villages and hamlets that united to form the city.

Page 12

Chapter Two

CANADA'S CROSSROADS

What a long road it has been …and train track, and air corridor and shipping lane, too. From the days when Aboriginal and European explorers and traders travelled the Credit River by canoe, Mississauga has been a transportation hub.

Page 28

Chapter Three

WORKING WORLD

Today, Mississauga is one of Canada's leading business centres. The city boasts some 20,000 businesses and is home to more head offices of Canadian corporations than all but four cities in the country.

Page 38

Chapter Four

PLANNING FOR GREATNESS

In a city that's home to some of the country's top corporations, one of the best-run businesses in Mississauga is … the City of Mississauga. With financial discipline, strategic vision, and service ethic, Mississauga is, indeed, a model of civic management.

Page 48

Chapter Five

PLAY TIME

Mississauga has always known how to enjoy leisure time, and it's home to some of best recreation opportunities anywhere—for all interests and ages, from pre-schoolers to seniors.

Page 58

Chapter Six

THAT'S ENTERTAINMENT!

Mississauga has reached a critical phase in its development, marked by an incredible range of cultural options, from galleries to the theatre, concerts to clubs, where people here can turn to stimulate, entertain and enthrall themselves.

Page 68

Chapter Seven

TO YOUR HEALTH

Take the pulse of wellness in Mississauga, and you find innovative hospitals, community programs that help residents prevent illness, and a flourishing local pharmaceutical sector that's discovering new ways to treat and prevent diseases.

Page 78

Chapter Eight

SCHOOL OF THOUGHT

The high quality of education in Mississauga, all through the years and in all its forms, is one reason why the people of this city are positioned to meet the challenges of the 21st century as members of the workforce and simply as citizens.

Page 84

❖

BUILDING ON EXCELLENCE

A quality, culturally diverse environment; a winning spirit; an unprecedented story of civic success; and an ideal home for business and industry. That's Mississauga.

On behalf of the Board of Directors of the Mississauga Board of Trade, I am pleased to present to you *Mississauga: Building on Excellence*, a book whose spectacular images and engaging copy harness the spirit of Mississauga, Ontario.

Within these pages, it is our sincere hope that you will experience the quality, texture and healthy pulse of this extraordinary city. We are rich in wonderful people, progressive partnerships, exciting opportunities, economic diversity and commercial vitality. As you enjoy this book, you will come to understand what makes Mississauga one of the most remarkable cities in the world, and why our future is so bright.

The sun has risen on a new century, and this is an exciting time for Mississauga. Those of us who live here know and appreciate the warmth and friendless of our people, respect the diversity of our traditions and heritage, honour the leaders who navigated the city to greatness, and look forward to many opportunities for a prosperous future.

I am proud to be a part of this unique and dynamic community.

The Mississauga Board of Trade is pleased to offer this book and hopes that it will provide a glimpse of the heart and soul of our city. At the same time, we hope that lifelong and newer residents alike will gain a new perspective by seeing our city through someone else's eyes, to perhaps rediscover the reasons that make Mississauga such a great place to live, work and do business. But most of all, a city to enjoy.

John W. Wouters
Chairman of the Board
Mississauga Board of Trade

Photo by Michael Scholz

Introduction

BLESSED BY GEOGRAPHY...AND RICH IN HISTORY

*P*hilip Cody wouldn't believe his eyes today. Neither would Timothy Street, Jacob Cook, or Richard Halliday. You mean *this* is Mississauga?

You could forgive their amazement.

In 1806, Cody became one of the first newcomers to the land. This was shortly after four Chiefs of the Mississaugas, an Ojibwa Tribe, agreed to sell to the Crown the southern part of the Mississauga Tract, some 70,784 acres. On the land where Dundas Street and Cawthra Road now meet, Cody built an inn for settlers and travellers. It was an ambitious goal in an area that, back then, was populated mostly by majestic oak and pine trees.

Who could have envisioned that enough "settlers" would flock here to make Mississauga the sixth largest city in Canada—a robust community of over 600,000, projected to grow to 780,000.

Timothy Street and Jacob Cook were among the community's early entrepreneurs, Street opening a sawmill and Cook operating a stagecoach mail service. They were such influential figures that the villages of Streetsville and Cooksville, both of which would one day become part of Mississauga, would be named in their honour.

These fathers of commerce would be astonished to see Mississauga's position today—the centre of Canada's largest consumer and industrial market, boasting 20,000 widely diversified businesses and the head offices of many of the country's top companies.

Richard Halliday arrived in 1819, and the farming area where he settled was eventually named for his native village of Malton, England. This was fertile land, particularly suitable to growing grain. The introduction of the Grand Trunk Railroad in 1854 provided access to nearby markets for local farmers, enhancing the area's prosperity and appeal.

Little could Halliday have known that transportation would play such a key role in Mississauga's rise—that Mississauga would become home to the country's busiest airport and the fourth busiest in North America, and would contain the greatest concentration of major highways in Canada.

A former Mayor of Mississauga, Martin Dobkin, once said the city was "blessed by geography." The city's strategic location does offer undeniable advantages. Mississauga lies just west of Toronto, along the banks of the Credit River, and on some of Canada's most desirable real estate. Seventy per cent of the buying power in Canada and the United States—over 125 million people—is within a day's drive. And 2.4 million of these people live no more than 20 kilometres from downtown Mississauga.

But Mississauga's success isn't just an accident of geography. It's the product of careful planning and the rich heritage of the numerous towns, villages and hamlets that united to form the city—a whole that's far greater than the sum of its parts.

Mississauga was only incorporated as a city in 1974, but it has a long and proud past and an even brighter future.

To take the measure of Mississauga, you must look at the vibrancy of its neighbourhoods and its infrastructure—what links the city, as well as the way the people and civic government do business—how the city works, the range of recreation and entertainment options—how the city plays. and at the quality of the health and education systems—how the city nurtures its bodies and minds.

By all of these measures, Mississauga is one of the most appealing, hospitable cities in Canada.

•Mississauga doubled in size in the 1980s and again in the 1990s and features a richly diverse business and civic life.

•The city exhibits all of the energy and gusto you would expect from a community that has grown so quickly.

•Mississauga is also one of the most affluent in Ontario's "Golden Horseshoe", with the highest standards in education, housing, recreation facilities, policing and health care.

•Mississauga has been proven statistically to be the safest of all the largest cities in Canada.

•Mississauga consistently boasts $1 billion a year in development.

•Despite its rapid rise, Mississauga has retained its local character and charms.

•Mississauga is a city filled with a highly skilled work force, nearly 70 percent of whom have post-secondary education.

•Mississauga, often observed to be run like a corporation by admirers, is debt-free, with a handsome surplus and lower taxes than neighbouring communities.

•Mississauga, as in Cody's day, embraces settlers and travellers from all corners of the world, and is still filled with "pioneers"—the entrepreneurs and artists, the distribution managers and pharmaceutical researchers, the retailers and university professors, the aerospace engineers and city planners—who are looking to blaze new trails in Mississauga's new century.

Photo by Michael Scholz

Chapter One

❖

_____

FRIENDS AND NEIGHBOURS

_____

Mississauga's success isn't just an accident of geography. It's the product of careful planning and the rich heritage of the numerous towns, villages and hamlets that united to form the city—a whole that's far greater than the sum of its parts. Photo by Michael Scholz.

When Ron Lenyk was a teenager growing up in the Sherway area of the Applewood subdivision in the 1960s, he knew where he belonged. "You talked about coming from your neighbourhood, coming from Sherway. There was tremendous pride in the neighbourhoods."

"Today, I'm also proud to say I'm from Mississauga," adds Lenyk, now Publisher of *The Mississauga News*. "Each community in the city is unique in its own way, and that's what made Mississauga so strong when it all came together."

Canada has been described as a "community of communities," a sentiment that could also apply to Mississauga.

"Cities traditionally grow from the inside out—we grew from the outside in," says Gay Peppin, Executive Director of Heritage Mississauga.

Mississauga's rich tapestry is woven from the fabric of many villages and towns, each with its own appeal. While Mississauga became a city in 1974, this community's story starts thousands of years ago when, archaeologists tell us, Aboriginal peoples inhabited this area.

By 1700, an Ojibwa group, the *Mississaugas*, called the Credit River Valley home. Soon the French and then the British, who had established posts around Lake Ontario, were trading with the Mississaugas, all of which lead to a momentous trade at the dawn of the 19th century. For 1,000 pounds sterling, the British Crown gained the "Mississauga Tract"—the lands along Lake Ontario between Etobicoke Creek and Burlington Bay.

Mississauga enjoys four distinct and wonderfully defined seasons, each imparting its own special beauty to the surrounding landscape. Crisp autumn air and shorter days turn the city's foliage into a brilliant display of fall color, one that gradually fades into the whiteness and chilly days of winter.
Photos by Michael Scholz

The Mississaugas did retain strips of land on either side of
the Credit River, which was surveyed in 1806 (and which later
passed on to the government too). So began an influx of immi-
grants and settlers into villages that became known collectively
as Toronto Township—the forerunner of Mississauga. "One of
the best settled townships in the Home District...large portion
of excellent land...a number of well cultivated farms," is how
the *Canadian Gazetteer* described the area in 1846. Here are
sketches of the branches of the Mississauga family tree.

Streetsville was the township's oldest village, a prosperous
milling and commercial centre. It featured the township's first
brick home (owned by Timothy Street, the village's namesake),
and first grammar school. If Timothy Street is Streetsville's
father, its favourite daughter is Hazel McCallion. This former

The cold days of winter give way to spring's mild temperatures. By late May, parks and gardens throughout the city are bursting with color and teeming with new life. By summer, warm temperatures lure people outdoors to enjoy the season's green facade. Photos by Michael Scholz.

Streetsville mayor went on to become Mayor of Mississauga—and one the longest-serving mayors in Canadian history.

Port Credit made its mark as a harbour for grain and lumber exports. Government Inn, the first permanent structure here, pre-dates Toronto Township and was built in 1798 as a way station for travellers. In the 19th century, Port Credit was a haven for "stonehookers"—people who collected shale from the bottom of Lake Ontario for use by the building trades.

Clarkson was named after Warren Clarkson, who arrived from New Brunswick around 1808. His family ran the general store and post office for years. The soil and weather here made for outstanding fruit crops. In fact, in the early 20th century Clarkson was the "Strawberry Capital of Canada."

Cooksville, in the heart of Toronto Township, eventually supplanted Streetsville as the site of the Town Hall. This centre for civic, industrial and commercial interests was home to Mississauga's first municipal offices, the central library, school board offices, and various federal and provincial ministries.

The quality of life in Mississauga can also be measured by the city's shops, restaurants, markets and bakeries and all of the other things that help enhance daily life in the city. Given Mississauga's proximity to local farms, it's not unusual to see farmers markets and roadside fruit stands overflowing with fresh produce and homemade goods. Photo by Michael Scholz.

Dixie developed around a government-owned tollbooth. It was named for Dr. Beaumont Dixie, who donated money to create the Union Chapel, a centre of the village's social and cultural life that still stands today.

Erindale's busy village life revolved around the mills, farms, post office, chair factory, and brewery. Also known as Springfield, it became a popular stop for travellers making the trek between Toronto and Hamilton.

Meadowvale was formed by the arrival of a caravan of Irish settlers from New York in 1819. While agriculture and milling were the main trades, Meadowvale was also an artists' haven a century ago. In 1980, it became Ontario's first heritage conservation district.

Malton played a key role in the township's agricultural life as a distribution hub for grain shipments in the 19th century. Today, it's known more for its skies than its soil. In 1937, the Toronto Harbour Commission selected 13 farms adjacent to the village for an airport, now Pearson International Airport, launching Malton's shift to an industrial centre.

Vigorous and enduring communities all—and in 1968 they entered a new chapter when the villages of Toronto Township, except Port Credit and Streetsville, united to became the Town of Mississauga. Six years later, all three towns amalgamated to become the City of Mississauga. But the old

communities weren't relegated to dusty old maps. They survive in the sense of identification that residents still hold.

"They say a chain is only as strong as its weakest link. Well, Mississauga is strong because each neighbourhood has such a strong identity," says Lenyk.

As one magazine profile noted, the very individuality of the former villages has created "the diverse, harmonious nature of Mississauga that has established it as a major Canadian city."

Evidence of community pride is everywhere, in events that evoke Mississauga's traditional heritage, like the Streetsville Founders Bread and Honey Festival, and in gatherings that celebrate the city's more recent heritage, like the Carassauga Festival of Cultures.

Mississauga has always been a city where people from across Canada and the world have felt at home. It was true during the early pioneer days; it was true in the post-war immigration boom, when new arrivals from Italy and Portugal found work in the brickyards of Cooksville and Streetsville; and it's true today, with Mississauga's large Chinese and East Indian communities, and enclaves of just about any other cultural group you can name.

Echoes of Mississauga's past live on in such historical places as the Bradley Museum, a heritage site that offers a glimpse at life in the 1800s.
Photos by Michael Scholz.

Mississauga's rich tapestry is woven from the fabric of many villages and towns, each with its own appeal. Photo by Michael Scholz.

There's a home and a neighborhood to suit every taste and income in Mississauga, whether it's a new house in a new subdivision, an apartment in the city, or an antique home in an historical neighborhood. Photo by Michael Scholz.

"Our diverse population adds to the strength of the community," says Lenyk. "At Carassauga, it's amazing to see how people from all over the world are the best of friends in Mississauga."

The city has become "a reception area for newcomers," says Lynn Petrushack, who runs the Dixie Bloor Neighbourhood Centre. In this part of town, there are neighbors from Vietnam and Poland, China and Pakistan, Korea and Sri Lanka, India and the former Yugoslavia. "People come from all shores of the world, and Dixie Bloor is the beach," quips Petrushack.

Apart from its ethnic diversity, Mississauga is a city of contrasts. At one end of town, you can browse the quaint shops of Port Credit. At another, you can marvel at Square One, one of North America's largest shopping centres, with 1.6 million square feet of retail space. At one end of town, there's the elegance of the early 20th century in the Benares Historic House, thought to be the inspiration for the famous *Whiteoaks of Jalna* novels by Mazo de la Roche. At another, you find City Centre's courtly condominiums of the 21st century.

"In some ways, Mississauga has the best of both worlds," says Rick Drennan, Editor of the *Mississauga Business Times*. "Some people are attracted

to the older neighbourhoods, with their leafy and settled atmosphere, to feel a connection with the past. Then you have the newer areas with thousands of homes, like north of Dundas and west of Highway 10, that are well planned."

In fact, with reasonable housing prices, loads of amenities, top school and health systems, extensive transportation links, and relatively low property taxes, Mississauga has some of the highest home building activity in Southern Ontario.

Drennan himself grew up in the Lakeview area in the 1950s and '60s. He has fond memories of running around the fields and hills of the old "Rifle Range," a former training ground for World War II soldiers. "That was our playpen." Today, he still feels a strong sense of neighbourhood involvement, like a series of mini communities within a larger one—"That's what makes Mississauga different from other cities."

For all the contrasts, Mississauga stands out just as much for what residents have in common—a desire to build a community that values the contributions of all citizens, that treasures its green space, that's safe, and that places a premium on quality of life.

The presence of water helped make Mississauga the thriving, accessible city it is today, and the Mississauga Waterfront Trail, with its sheer beauty and maritime atmosphere, is one of the city's biggest lures. Photo by Michael Scholz.

While the city is still relatively young, Mississauga is at an important phase in its development—a time when the city is truly coming together. Peppin sees it in events like Canada Day celebrations at the Civic Centre, which each year draw thousands, and "rally people from all over the city."

People here hardly need an excuse to party. Throughout the year, Mississaugans gather for children's festivals and outdoor art shows, charity walkathons and waterfront festivals, jazz festivals and the Santa Claus Parade, the Great Ontario Salmon Hunt and the annual New Year's Day levee at the Civic Centre.

Peppin also sees civic pride in the development of new landmarks. "Community centres are great for a particular area, but buildings like the Living Arts Centre and the Hershey Centre are for the whole city. We're starting to see those unifying forces," she says.

"In some ways, Mississauga has the best of both worlds," says Rick Drennan, Editor of the Mississauga Business Times. *"Some people are attracted to the older neighbourhoods, with their leafy and settled atmosphere, to feel a connection with the past. Then you have the newer areas with thousands of homes, like north of Dundas and west of Highway 10, that are well planned."*
Photo by Michael Scholz.

"What makes any city distinctive is its heritage," she continues. "Heritage is up to the moment, not just something that happened 100 years ago. People need a pride of place to participate in making it a better place. And people who live here feel Mississauga is a distinct place."

Just how has the city changed? Petrushack recalls that in the mid-1970s, she would drive to Mississauga to buy eggs right from a farmer. Now she lives in that former farmland, which in a generation has become the middle of a bustling metropolis.

"Everything here is fresh and exciting, with so much new life," says Petrushack. "It's fun to be part of a community that's changing and growing so much." ❖

Welcome Wagon Ltd. has been Canada's neighbourhood tradition since 1930. As a public service, Welcome Wagon distributes literature for civic, cultural and social organizations to Mississauga's newcomers. Photo courtesy of Welcome Wagon Ltd.

As Mississauga expands, so does its neighborhoods and subdivisions, which have expanded steadily in recent years to make Mississauga a community of 600,000 people—Canada's sixth largest city. Photo by Michael Scholz.

Whether old or new, urban or suburban, Mississauga's neighborhoods are safe, clean, and beautiful—models of excellence for communities throughout North America. Photo by Michael Scholz.

Chapter Two

CANADA'S CROSSROADS

Location and an excellent transportation infrastructure have established Mississauga as one of the most connected cities in Canada and one of North America's vital hubs of commerce and transportation.
Photo by Bill Bachmann.

What a long road it has been…and train track, and air corridor and shipping lane too. From the days when Aboriginal and European explorers and traders travelled the Credit River by canoe, Mississauga has been a transportation hub.

In the early 1800s, it might take a rider and horse a day to get between here and neighbouring Toronto—a transportation marvel. Today, it's a short hop from your Mississauga office to Pearson International Airport, and an 80-minute flight from New York. Or you load your freight with one of Mississauga's trucking companies, and in an hour it's at the U.S. border. You could say that Mississauga's connections—by land, air, rail, and sea—have led its prominence.

"Our transportation infrastructure is the number one reason for the city's industrial, commercial and residential growth," states Alan Boughton, President of Mississauga-based Trailcon Leasing.

Boughton, who has chaired the Transportation and Airport committees for the Mississauga Board of Trade, says the city's superior links suggest the chicken-and-egg question. Strong transportation attracts business, which spurs people to move here, which draws more business, which increases the population, which…you get the picture.

Any major city should boast first-rate transportation. But Mississauga's network is more notable than most, making this city, in many ways, the crossroads of Canada.

On the Road Again

Which North American city is served by the most highways? L.A.? Chicago? Guess again. Seven major multi-lane highways cross Mississauga offering easy access across the city and region to other points in the Ontario and down to the U.S. That makes for more convenient commutes and, for industry, timesaving shipments.

Highway 401 is Canada's busiest thoroughfare, running from Windsor to Quebec, which has six interchanges through Mississauga. The Queen Elizabeth Way (QEW) connects the Greater Toronto Area and provides entry to New York State. Highway 403 connects the QEW with Highway 401 and provides an east/west link through the centre of Mississauga. Highway 427 links Toronto with Mississauga, and Highway 409 provides a link from the 401 and 427 to Pearson Airport. Highway 410 serves the city's industrial area west of the airport and provides a link north through Mississauga from the 403 and 401. Highway 407, the world's first all-electronic toll road, spans the northern section of the

Greater Toronto Area, including Mississauga's northern and western boundaries. This technologically advanced toll highway allows for faster movement of goods throughout the region, yet another reason why so many businesses locate in Mississauga.

With Mississauga's access to all these highways, great arterial roads, and strategic location, it's no surprise that the city is a distribution mecca. In fact, the Ontario Trucking Association has more members in Mississauga by far than any other city. Check the Mississauga Yellow Pages, and you'll find scores of listings for truck terminals, long-distance carriers, local delivery and courier companies, warehouses, container companies, freight forwarders and customs brokers.

Seven major multi-lane highways-more than any other city in North America—transect Mississauga, thereby providing easy access to Detroit, Chicago, New York, Boston, Washington, D.C., Montreal, Quebec City and beyond. Photo by Michael Scholz.

And no wonder. Some 125 million people are within a day's drive of Mississauga, including Detroit, Chicago, New York, Boston, Washington, D.C., Montreal and Quebec City. And Minneapolis, St. Louis, Nashville and Atlanta are within a two-day drive. Consider this amazing fact—more trade travels over the Ambassador Bridge between Ontario and Michigan, much of it originating in Mississauga, than between all of the U.S. and Japan.

"If you're in transportation and you're not in Mississauga, you're not where you should be," says Boughton, whose trailers carry over half of Ontario's food.

Government continues to strongly support the highway system's development and maintenance, recognizing that world-class highways are literally a road to economic success.

Mississauga's access to several major highways and great arterial roads, together with its strategic location, have turned the city into a distribution mecca. Photo by Michael Scholz.

Something in the Air

If Mississauga's highways have helped pave the way for the city's affluence and influence, so has the presence of Pearson International Airport. Canada's busiest, it accounts for one-third of passenger air traffic in the country. About 28 million people pass through its gates each year, a number that's expected to rise to over 33 million by 2005, and over 50 million by 2015.

Pearson is already among the world's top 25 airports, and is the fourth largest gateway to North America. Some 55 airlines fly out of three terminals to over 100 destinations in 44 countries. The airport also handles 350,000 tonnes of cargo and mail annually.

Mississauga residents and companies find the airport's proximity, and its connections to major cities worldwide, highly convenient. From Pearson, Montreal is 65 minutes away, Chicago 95 minutes, and Vancouver under five hours.

The presence of Pearson International Airport, Canada's busiest airport, accounts for one-third of passenger air traffic in the country.

Atlanta is a two-hour flight, and Dallas is a little over three. You can be in L.A. and Mexico City in about five hours, and London and Paris in seven.

Today, the airport is taking steps to fly even higher. Pearson is in the midst of a $4.4 billion project to completely revamp the airport and create a sparkling new terminal, with phase one due for completion in 2007.

As air travel increases, Pearson will continue to be one of the most important passenger and goods terminals on the globe—and an engine of the Mississauga economy.

On the Right Track

Mississauga's strategic transportation advantage extends to the rail lines, with easy access for daily commuters, long-distance passengers and industrial shippers. Canada's two chief railways, Canadian National and Canadian Pacific, both have main lines crossing Mississauga. Both also provide inter-modal services from terminals just north of Mississauga (CN in Brampton), just east of Mississauga (CP in Etobicoke), and northeast of Mississauga (CP in Vaughan).

For inter-city and long-distance passenger service, VIA Rail operates out of Union Station, just 18 km east of Mississauga. And GO Transit, operated by the Government of Ontario, provides commuter train service across the Greater Toronto Area, including three train lines (and several GO bus routes) through Mississauga. That gives residents convenient rail access to jobs outside of the city's borders, and lets others easily commute to jobs within Mississauga.

Out to Sea

In the 1830s, Port Credit began to build up a major harbour, the only one in the township. With a couple of wharves and a warehouse, this was an export point for grain and lumber, and became the centre of a shipbuilding industry.

Today, Mississauga lies between two of the largest Great Lakes ports—the Port of Toronto, 18 km east, and the Port of Hamilton, 33 km west. Together, they handle 14 million tonnes of cargo a year and have 1.3 million square feet of warehousing. Located on Lake Ontario, Mississauga has direct access to all lake ports and to the Atlantic Ocean via the St. Lawrence Seaway.

The Wheels on the Bus

What has an annual ridership of 24 million, and travels 18 million kilometres a year—enough to get to the moon and back 22 times? The answer is Mississauga Transit.

Approximately 28 million people pass through the gates of Lester B. Pearson International Airport each year, a figure that is expected to nearly double in less than 15 years. Photo courtesy of L.B. Pearson International Airport.

Mississauga's strategic transportation advantage extends to the rail lines, with easy access for daily commuters, long-distance passengers and industrial shippers. Canada's two chief railways, Canadian National and Canadian Pacific, both have main lines crossing Mississauga. *Photo by Michael Scholz.*

The award-winning public transit system blankets the city with more than 300 vehicles, about 55 routes, and over 3,000 bus stops. Beside the routes throughout the city, Mississauga Transit offers connections with the Toronto Transit Commission, Brampton Transit, Oakville Transit and all GO Transit stations. A special City Centre shuttle, a joint venture between the city and major developers, also provides free bus service through the City Centre area.

Bill Cunningham, Director of Transit for Mississauga Transit, agrees that the city's extensive road network is a key reason why Mississauga has experienced such rapid growth. To him, a vibrant public transit system is a major part of the mix.

"That's something that helps attract business to the city, for one. Companies expect the buses to be able to drop people at their door," says Cunningham. "In any mature city, you should have choices in your enablers of mobility. And public transit is an important choice."

I Get Around

The City of Mississauga, the Region of Peel and the Province of Ontario are keenly aware of the transportation system's significance to the community's economic and social viability. All three levels of government have slated

Mississauga Transit operates more than 300 vehicles on more than 50 routes, and moves 2.4 million commuters annually to their destinations. Photo by Michael Scholz.

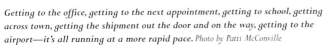

Getting to the office, getting to the next appointment, getting to school, getting across town, getting the shipment out the door and on the way, getting to the airport—it's all running at a more rapid pace. Photo by Patti McConville

ambitious transportation improvements over the first decade of the century. In recent years, the city itself has committed as much of one-third of its capital works budget to road construction projects.

"Maintaining your transportation infrastructure is extremely important," says Angus McDonald, Mississauga's Commissioner of Transportation and Works. "On both sides, the movement of goods and the movement of people, I think we have a very good network."

In today's mobile world, everyone and everything is looking to move faster. Getting to the office, getting to the next appointment, getting to school, getting across town, getting the shipment out the door and on the way, getting to the airport—it's all running at a more rapid pace.

Part of being a "city on the move" is helping people to be literally on the move. Mississauga's sophisticated transportation network continues to make the city appealing, whether you live here, work here, or are just passing through—quickly and efficiently, of course. ❖

Sitting on Lake Ontario between two of the largest Great Lakes ports—the Port of Toronto and the Port of Hamilton—Mississauga has direct access to all lake ports and to the Atlantic Ocean via the St. Lawrence Seaway.

Chapter Three

WORKING WORLD

Mississauga is one of Canada's leading centres of commercial activity, boasting 20,000 businesses—11,000 of which are in the industrial and commercial sector, and 9,000 in retail. Photo by Michael Scholz.

❦

Despite its manufacturing industries, Mississauga has never fallen victim to urban blight. Instead it has reached and maintains a happy balance between the city's industry and its green spaces. Photo by Michael Scholz.

Mississauga is home to more head offices of Canadian corporations than all but four cities in the country. Photo by Michael Scholz.

If you want to understand how Mississauga has evolved, just look at the working life of its people. For early settlers in the 1800s, life revolved largely around farming. A small business meant a blacksmith shop, a tavern or a general store. And "big industry?" Maybe a sawmill or wool mill. Even into the early part of the 20th century, much of the area remained farmland.

It wasn't until the post-war period that the city's industrial base began to strengthen, with a focus on the aerospace industry. Even then, people had to largely travel to neighbouring cities for jobs in manufacturing, finance, and business services.

"Chemicals help to make our lives more comfortable and safer every day in the areas of personal and health care, food, protection and clothing. We firmly believe that industrial development must be supported by constant dedication to the respect and safety of our business and residential neighbours within the surrounding environment, which is why Rhodia is a long-standing supporter of the Responsible Care initiative around the globe, and is committed to improve safety, and protect health and the environment."

John Di Massimo
Vice-President & CFO
Rhodia Canada Inc.

At least 1,500 international corporations make Mississauga their Canadian home base, including 1,000 or so American firms, and about 100 from each the United Kingdom, Germany and Japan. Photo by Michael Scholz.

Mississauga is well known for its attractive economic climate. According to a recent study, the city ranked thirteenth among cities all over the world for business cost competitiveness. Photo by Michael Scholz.

Mississauga is able to meet any company's most demanding telecommunications needs, with a more sophisticated infrastructure than those of many nearby municipalities. No wonder Mississauga has attracted so many technology-based companies. Photo by Michael Scholz.

How Things Have Changed

Today, Mississauga is one of Canada's leading business centres. The city boasts some 20,000 businesses, 11,000 in the industrial and commercial sector, and 9,000 in retail.

Mississauga is home to more head offices of Canadian corporations than all but four cities in the country.

At least 1,500 international corporations make Mississauga their Canadian home base, including 1,000 or so American firms, and about 100 each from the U.K., Germany and Japan.

While the business base is diverse enough that no one sector dominates, Mississauga is a leader in a number of industries—information technology, biomedical and pharmaceutical technologies, aerospace, and distribution and logistics. These are among the most booming sectors of the economy, positioning Mississauga well for future job growth.

Perhaps most impressive, Mississauga, a former bedroom community, is now a net *importer* of jobs.

How did Mississauga achieve such an incredible transformation? True, the city's quality housing and schools, first rate health and medical services, and abundant recreation and arts opportunities are all appealing to any business—or businessperson—who is thinking of moving here. But to David Gordon, Managing Director and COO of the Mississauga Board of Trade, the prime factor in Mississauga's rise as a business powerhouse is the city's transportation links.

"In every sense of the word, that's what drives the economy," says Gordon.

Consider the city's easy access to global and local markets and suppliers. Because Mississauga is home to Canada's busiest airport, both goods and business travellers can move quickly between local companies and any point in the world.

Back on the ground, Mississauga's extensive network of highways keep people and goods moving and the city connected. In fact, says Gordon, "More major highways criss-cross Mississauga than any other municipality in North America."

The highway system and Mississauga's strategic location—in the centre of Canada's major consumer and industrial market, and just 90 minutes from the U.S. border—have made Mississauga the trucking and distribution capital of Canada.

Mississauga's transportation advantage for business isn't just by air and land, but by rail and sea as well. Canada's two principal railways have main lines crossing the city, accommodating freight transport, and Mississauga's location on the northern shore of Lake Ontario—between two of the largest ports on the Great Lakes—gives local businesses access to all lake ports and to the Atlantic Ocean via the St. Lawrence Seaway.

But transportation and convenient access to key markets, while vitally important, aren't the only reasons for
Mississauga's success as a business location. Why else do
companies like Glaxo Wellcome and Nortel, Ready Bake
Foods and General Electric, Boeing and Microsoft, Xerox
and Astra Pharma, and Air Canada and Bell Mobility call
Mississauga home?

"Just look at the skills of our labour force," says Larry
Petovello, Director of Economic Development for the City
of Mississauga. Nearly 70 per cent of the city's workforce
has post-secondary education. And with eight universities
and 10 technical colleges located within commuting

*Bales of hay on the outskirts of the city form an intriguing juxtaposition of the
city's old and new economies.* Photo by Michael Scholz.

*Nearly 70 per cent of the city's workforce has post-secondary education. And with
eight universities and 10 technical colleges located within commuting distance,
local companies have ongoing access to a large pool of highly trained employees.*

The highly active development industry has kept lease rates and land prices reasonable within the city, in itself very attractive to businesses. But Mississauga also has the lowest electricity rates in the Greater Toronto Area, and Hydro Mississauga keeps finding ways to reduce its rates even further. Natural gas is also readily available to local industries at about the lowest prices in North America. Photos by Michael Scholz.

distance of Mississauga, local companies have ongoing access to a large pool of highly trained employees.

Listen to Ichiro Joh, President of the NTN Bearing Corporation of Canada. The firm is a key supplier to the OEM automotive industry, so locating in Mississauga was important just to be less than an hour from Ford, General Motors, Honda, Toyota, Chrysler and Cami (GM/Suzuki) assembly plants. But Joh says the presence of a skilled workforce is even more important.

"Perhaps the largest factor in our successful manufacturing growth in Mississauga is our ability to expand our output while maintaining exacting quality standards," he says. "At first we were concerned as to whether a locally hired work force could meet these standards. But we were pleased to be proven wrong. Now the most complex overhauls and maintenance of precision equipment are carried out by our Canadian staff."

In all, Mississauga's employers have access to not only the city's 335,000 employees, but to a pool of more than 2 million workers across the Greater Toronto Region.

The quality of Mississauga's workforce is a vital part of the city's economic success.
Photo by John Borge.

Mississauga's employers have access to not only the city's 335,000 employees, but to a pool of more than 2 million workers across the Greater Toronto Region.
Photo by Michael Scholz.

The continuing population growth of the city and region only expands the available labour force. The Economic Development Office predicts that, ultimately, 540,000 people will work in Mississauga.

Petovello also points to the city's pro-business government. It has been said that Mississauga itself is run like a business, and Brian Donovan, General Manager for Robert Allen Fabrics (Canada) Inc., agrees. This distributor of upholstery and drapery fabrics moved their Canadian head office and call centre to Mississauga from Montreal in 1994.

"We not only found a great location close to Highway 401 and minutes from the airport, but we were amazed at the City's no-nonsense way of doing business, particularly the low taxes and the lack of red tape," says Donovan.

The city's commitment to excellence and sound financial management have led to high quality municipal services and low taxes—two things that affect the decisions of businesses to locate or expand their operations in a particular city. In fact, Mississauga's property taxes are among the lowest in Ontario.

In other areas, Mississauga is just as attractive an economic climate for businesses. "We rank Thirteenth among cities all across the world for business cost competitiveness," says Gordon, citing a study by KPMG.

For instance, the highly active development industry has kept lease rates and land prices quite reasonable. Mississauga's highly reliable electric power has the lowest rates in the Greater Toronto Area, and Enersource Hydro Mississauga Corporation keeps finding ways to reduce rates even further. Natural gas is also readily available to local industries at about the lowest prices in North America.

"Moving to Mississauga was an important step in making needed improvements to our bottom line," says John Gates, General Manager, Sunbeam Corporation Canada Inc. The manufacturer of household appliances moved their Canadian head office and distribution centre to Mississauga from Toronto in 1994, seeking more efficient distribution and lower operating costs.

"It costs less to do business here, as we make substantial savings on taxes and electricity compared to our previous location," adds Gates. "And by remaining in the area, we retained our existing employees and have a great work force to draw on as we expand."

Overall, the city's infrastructure couldn't be more accommodating to business. Along with the presence of the airport, the major highways, the railways and the nearby ports, Mississauga is served by a well-maintained local road system and extensive public transit.

The city's abundant water supply is carried by an infrastructure that was built in anticipation of future expansion. All residential and industrial subdivisions are fully serviced for water and sanitary sewers.

Mississauga is also able to meet any company's most demanding telecommunications needs, with a more sophisticated infrastructure than those of many nearby municipalities. No wonder Mississauga has attracted so many technology-based companies.

Where to locate all of the companies who are flocking to Mississauga? No problem. The city has the largest supply of modern, high quality, industrial land and buildings in the Greater Toronto Area. About 5,000 acres are still to be developed for business, and over 50 private sector business parks offer a terrific choice of locations for new arrivals and business expansions.

To Robert Gordon, President of Oracle Corporation Canada, the city's ability to accommodate rapid expansion, its tax savings, the airport, "the excellent highway connections" and "the quality of the workforce" all combine to lead to one conclusion. "This is the best place to do business in the Toronto area," he states.

The city's businesses also have a strong advocate in the Mississauga Board of Trade, one of the largest such boards in the country. The "voice of business" in Mississauga, as it bills itself, helps members broaden their scope and realize new opportunities through management seminars, business development networking, alliances with other industry associations, and lobbying efforts. In so doing, the MBOT creates an environment in which Mississauga businesses can compete and prosper, locally and internationally.

The MBOT's Gordon notes that while the city's infrastructure, social and economic benefits attract businesses from around Canada and the world, the ever-increasing business presence in turn helps spur Mississauga's population growth.

"When people who live outside Mississauga come here to work, they see all the great things that the city has to offer," he says. "People say, 'What a great place to raise a family.'" All of which makes Mississauga—for businesses and their employees alike—a destination of choice.❖

Information technology, biomedical and pharmaceutical technologies, aerospace, and distribution and logistics are industries that keep Mississauga as commercially dynamic as it is innovative. Standing on the forefront of the ever-expanding high-tech industry, Mississauga is positioned for future job growth. Photo by Michael Scholz.

Chapter Four

PLANNING FOR GREATNESS

Once a former bedroom community, Mississauga has emerged, with strategic planning and forward thinking, from the shadow of Toronto to become a major North American city in its own right and a net importer of jobs. Photo by Michael Scholz.

In a city that's home to some of the country's top corporations, one of the best-run businesses in Mississauga is…the City of Mississauga. Since its incorporation as a city 1974, Mississauga has been a model of civic management. The city is run with a financial discipline, a strategic vision, and a service ethic. This is where you'll hear politicians and city staff talk about residents as "customers"—and mean it.

How has the local government encouraged and sustained Mississauga's growth? And what kind of planning is ensuring that Mississauga will continue to thrive?

"We do run very much like a business," says Dave O'Brien, City Manager. "City council is like the board of directors, the mayor is the CEO, I'm like a chief operating officer, and the commissioners are like vice-presidents with their own portfolio."

Local "stockholders" have to be pleased with the organization's financial performance. While governments at all levels borrow to finance their expenditures, Mississauga has been debt-free since the 1970s. In fact, the city entered the new century with over $360 million in reserve funds to pay for future infrastructure. All this while managing lower industrial property taxes, in some cases dramatically lower, than the rates in neighbouring cities.

"We've stuck to a financial plan," says Janice Baker, Commissioner of Corporate Services for the City of Mississauga. "A long time ago, we adopted a pay-as-you-go policy. The city won't incur debt to finance capital projects. Your facility costs are cheaper in the long run, and you have more flexibility in managing your budget. Everything is open to you. And it's because of our financial health that we're able to maintain facilities and provide such a broad range of services at such a high level."

A key to Mississauga's rosy financial picture was a decision made early in the city's life to levy charges on developers. "Growth pays for growth," as Baker says. Many cities take that route today, but when Mississauga started it, the concept was novel. "The bulk of our reserve funds comes from development-related charges," O'Brien says. "That lets us have a very strategic capital plan. We know that three years from now, we'll have enough money to build 'X.' And in five years, we'll have enough to build 'Y.' And with that plan, you can begin to project your operating budget many years out."

Too many municipalities, he says, focus on capital project costs and downplay the ongoing operating costs. Not Mississauga. "We think long-term, and bring a business perspective to our decisions," O'Brien states. "I've worked for six cities, but never one like Mississauga, as competent in decision making, financial planning and strategic thinking."

Much of the credit for Mississauga's prudent management and rise as an urban force goes to Hazel McCallion. First elected as Mayor of Mississauga in 1978, she was returned to office in 1980, 1982, 1985, 1988, 1991, 1994, 1997 and 2000—an incredible record of unbroken faith. During her time in office, Mayor McCallion saw Mississauga grow from a city of 100,000, still with plenty of farmland, to a cosmopolitan community of more than 600,000.

In a city that's home to some of the country's top corporations, one of the best-run businesses in Mississauga is the City of Mississauga itself. Photo by Michael Scholz.

"She has put her personal stamp on Mississauga—caring, compassionate, strong policies, and not afraid to stick your neck out and lead," says O'Brien.

Mississauga's confidence and dogged pursuit of excellence reflects Mayor McCallion's own personality. She was the first woman to be elected President of the Streetsville and District Chamber of Commerce, the first woman Mayor of Streetsville, and the first woman Mayor of Mississauga. She has been so popular that, on more than one occasion, no one dared run against her, and when she did face opponents, she would routinely win over 90 per cent of the vote.

While she is Mississauga's champion, Mayor McCallion has also been a strong voice on key issues affecting the future of the entire region. In 1992, for instance, she established the Greater Toronto Area Mayors' Committee to work cooperatively for the region's economic prosperity. Countless provincial and federal committees and associations have also called on Mayor McCallion to lend her invaluable insight and experience.

The City of Mississauga, along with being well managed, is also a great place to work. In 2000, the city was recognized as one of the top 100 employers in Canada. That followed a national study of more than 30,000 companies and organizations. Only two other cities in Canada earned this distinction.

Richard Yerema, who wrote a book on Canada's top employers, calls Mississauga a municipal wonder. At a time when many city governments are downsizing or feeling the brunt of funding cuts, Mississauga is still expanding. "What's incredible about Mississauga is that it has managed tremendous growth exceptionally well," says Yerema.

Mississauga is a model of proper management and financial success. In fact, the city entered the new century with over $360 million in reserve funds to pay for future infrastructure. Photo by Michael Scholz.

HAZEL McCALLION
MAYOR

Much of the credit for Mississauga's prudent management and rise as an urban force goes to Hazel McCallion, who was first elected as Mayor of Mississauga in 1978, and returned to office in 1980, 1982, 1985, 1988, 1991, 1994, 1997 and 2000. Photo by Michael Scholz.

During her time in office, Mayor McCallion saw Mississauga grow from a city of 100,000, still with plenty of farmland, to a cosmopolitan community of more than 600,000. Photo by Michael Scholz.

With cranes and bulldozers dotting the landscape, growth is visible nearly everywhere in the city. Mississauga consistently had over $1 billion worth of construction activity a year, sometimes well over. Photo by Michael Scholz.

With City Council, staff, residents, businesses and other stakeholders working together, Mississauga will keep arriving at creative solutions to the challenges of modern urban life. Photo by Michael Scholz.

Photo by *Michael Scholz.*

A recent survey indicated Mississauga residents gave the city a 93 per cent satisfaction rating, by far the highest rating of all municipalities in the region. Photo by Michael Scholz.

Aside from being exceedingly well run, Mississauga is among the safest communities in Canada. Peel Regional Police is a progressive service, focusing on crime prevention and community policing, and boasting a crime clearance record well above national and provincial averages. Photo by Michael Scholz.

"We have excellent staff and work hard to attract and retain quality employees," notes O'Brien. "With high calibre staff, we can provide service excellence to our residents."

In fact, in a survey by an independent research group, Mississauga residents gave the city a 93 per cent satisfaction rating, by far the highest rating of all municipalities in the region.

Aside from being exceedingly well run, Mississauga is also the safest community in Canada. Peel Regional Police is a progressive service, focusing on crime prevention and community policing, and boasting a crime clearance record well above national and provincial averages. The service has earned numerous awards for quality in policing and has been certified by the prestigious Commission on Accreditation for Law Enforcement Agencies, a first for an Ontario police agency.

The city also has a professional Fire and Emergency Services Department, with one firefighter per 1,272 residents—above the national average—strong prevention activities, and an average response time of just four to five minutes.

Part of the city's success stems from the fact that, while it was knit together from several older communities, the City of Mississauga itself is relatively young. From the start, the city had a clear vision of the kind of modern community it wanted to be, and was disciplined enough to stick to that vision.

"We've gone through exhaustive exercises of planning the community in concert with the community," says Tom Mokrzycki, the city's Commissioner of Planning and Building.

The city has a professional Fire and Emergency Services Department, with one firefighter per 1,272 residents—above the national average—strong prevention activities, and an average response time of just four to five minutes.
Photo by Michael Scholz.

Mississauga's location between Toronto and the U.S. market has helped make the city attractive to business. That, in turn, spurs residential growth. Indeed, Mississauga has become a cosmopolitan city that residents are proud to call "home." *Photo by Michael Scholz.*

At the same time, Mississauga's strategic location—the major highways, Pearson International Airport, the frontage on the water, the railway lines, and the fact that it lies between Toronto and the U.S. market—has made the city attractive to business. That, in turn, spurs residential growth.

Cranes and bulldozers dot the Mississauga scenery. The city has consistently had over $1 billion worth of construction activity a year, sometimes well over. Mokrzycki notes that for several years running, Mississauga has ranked among the top three municipalities in Canada by construction activity. During a recent three-year period alone, Mississauga added 14,000 new homes, 15.6 million square feet of industrial space, 4.2 million square feet of office space, and 2.1 million square feet of retail space.

"We've ended up with a city where you can do anything you want—great theatre, restaurants, shopping, recreation—without having to leave. The community is becoming self-contained," says O'Brien. "We attend conferences all over the world on urban issues. And speakers always say that Mississauga is a leader."

Never a city to rest on its success, Mississauga is ready to respond to the challenges of the new millennium with a fresh strategic direction. It provides the framework for long-term growth and development, and includes input from dozens of stakeholder groups—from ratepayer and neighbourhood associations, to community agencies, to utilities.

This is nothing new for the city. Mississauga has been creating strategic plans since the early 1990s, to give the city corporation a focus and citizens an understanding of the city's vision for the future.

What kind of city does Mississauga want to be in the 21st century? Looking at the latest plan's 10 vision statements, it seeks to be 1) a distinct major Canadian city, with 2) the City Centre as the downtown and 3) distinct and recognizable communities. It will be a city with 4) a dynamic and diverse economic base, and 5) a transportation system which allows for safe and efficient movement. Mississauga will 6) provide the right services, delivered in a superior way, at a reasonable cost. It will be 7) an environmentally responsible community, 8) governed in an open and responsive manner. Finally, the city will 9) achieve excellence in public administration, and 10) offer a diversity of cultural opportunities

Each of these vision statements comes with specific objectives and the actions needed to reach them. The statements are then incorporated into the design and delivery of city programs and services, "guiding principles for the city's corporate decision making," states Mayor McCallion.

For instance, having "distinct and recognizable communities" depends on things like ensuring that new development is compatible, and preserving buildings, sites and landscapes of historical and architectural significance. And being "governed in an open and responsive manner" means you ensure the maximum opportunities for public participation.

Strategic management is an ongoing process. With City Council, staff, residents, businesses and other stakeholders working together, Mississauga will keep arriving at creative solutions to the challenges of modern urban life. As has been the case since the city's inception, civic planners will no doubt ensure that Mississauga will continue to be a community that people are proud to call home.❖

During a recent three-year period, Mississauga added 14,000 new homes, 15.6 million square feet of industrial space, 4.2 million square feet of office space, and 2.1 million square feet of retail space. Photo by Michael Scholz.

Chapter Five

❖

PLAY TIME

"Recreation is an essential component in making life livable, let alone making Mississauga more livable," says Paul Mitcham, the City of Mississauga's Commissioner of Community Services. Nearly twenty thousand recreational programs fill Mississauga's calendar annually.
Photo by Michael Scholz.

Looking to define the meaning of recreation? Just break down the word—re-creation. That's what we're doing when we indulge in any leisure pursuit, from a walk in the park to a pickup hockey game. We're literally re-creating ourselves, engaging our body and mind in an activity just for the stimulation and satisfaction it brings.

"Recreation is an essential component in making life livable, let alone making Mississauga more livable," says Paul Mitcham, the City of Mississauga's Commissioner of Community Services, which includes parks and recreation.

Mississauga has always known how to enjoy leisure time. Back in the 1800s, you might see local residents gather for quilting bees or berry picking, a game of lacrosse or a barn raising or perhaps ice sailing on the Credit River. Today, Mississauga is home to some of the best recreation opportunities anywhere, and residents and visitors take full advantage.

Start with Mississauga's extensive range of recreation programs—some 5,500 in the

Mississauga contains more than 425 parks comprising over 5,650 acres. New parkland is added all the time to keep up with residential growth and add to the city's green space. Photos by Michael Scholz.

summer, 5,000 in the winter, 4,200 in the fall and 3,700 in the spring. The programs generate 120,000 registrations a year, amazing in a city of 600,000.

Recreation programs are tailored to all interests and ages, from preschoolers to seniors, and are available at reasonable prices that encourage broad participation. Do you flip over gymnastics? Click your heels over dance? Have a ball playing soccer? Would you beat a path to go skiing? Or is tennis more your racket? Do fitness routines get you in a sweat? Or would you rather be in the swim?

The City of Mississauga provides all of these possibilities, and more, to fulfill your recreational urges in the most modern and well-maintained facilities. Consider what the city has to offer.

• Eighteen community centres, from major multi-functional facilities (pool, gym, library, etc.) to smaller single-use centres such as a lawn bowling club.
• Indoor ice-rink surfaces for skating, hockey and ringette, including Iceland Mississauga. This state-of-the-art facility features an arena with Olympic-size ice surface, three 300-seat arenas with professional-size ice surfaces, a pro shop, and a children's learning centre.

The city maintains more than 20 major trails totaling about 120 kilometres (over 70 miles) along stream valleys and through woodlots. The trails provide a safe, convenient and healthy way to navigate the city on foot or bicycle.
Photos by Michael Scholz.

- Ten indoor pools, including one with a two-storey flume slide, a 10,000-gallon whirlpool and 8 water-play splash pads.

- Seven fitness centres, with complete weight-training facilities, cycle, stair and rowing machines, aerobic gyms, and squash and racquetball courts.

- Over 425 parks, comprising over 5,650 acres. New parkland is added all the time to keep up with residential growth and add to the city's green space. The biggest project in development is Riverwood Gardens, to open in 2004, representing the largest remaining Carolinian forest in Canada and destined to be a major public garden attraction.

- 311 soccer fields and 273 baseball diamonds.

- Twenty major trails, along stream valleys and through woodlots, totaling about 120 kilometres (over 70 miles). They provide a safe, convenient and

When you consider that the Indian word Mississauga *means "river in the north of many mouths," it's no surprise that Mississaugans are drawn to the water as are these ducks.* Photo by Michael Scholz.

healthy way to navigate the city. "Trails are one of the most important parts of the recreation infrastructure, because anyone can use them, any time, whether walking, jogging, cycling, cross-country skiing or in-line skating," says Mitcham.

• A gymnastic training facility, established by the city in conjunction with Gymnastics Mississauga, which has led to the development of world-class competitors from the area.

• The Britannia Hills Golf Course, owned by the Region of Peel and operated by the City of Mississauga. This 18-hole course, designed in the Scottish style, provides a spectacular view of the surrounding neighbourhoods.

A few of the city's jewels deserve a closer look. The Hershey Centre, which opened in 1998, is Mississauga's sports and entertainment hub. The 5,400-seat facility, with capacity for 7,000 for some events, is home to the Mississauga IceDogs of the Ontario Hockey League, featuring the National Hockey League players of tomorrow. The IceDogs are partly owned by

Anglers from across Ontario, the border states, and even Europe say that some of the world's best salmon fishing is off of Port Credit, one reason why Mississauga has one of Lake Ontario's largest fleets of charter boats. Photo by Michael Scholz.

renowned Mississauga resident, former NHL coach, and broadcasting icon Don Cherry.

This versatile complex holds two rinks—the Hershey Centre Arena and a full-size community rink—for use by hockey leagues, figure skating clubs and community groups. Sports are only part of the attraction at the Hershey Centre, which has held every type of concert, family show, and trade and business exhibition imaginable.

"A venue like this says a lot about the city's growth," says Ken Noakes, Executive Director of the Hershey Centre. "It's a place where you can strive to play, support the home team, or cheer for your favourite form of entertainment, right in your own community. It helps round out the culture of the city."

The complex is located on 160 hectares of land, part of a major sports park development referred to as the Sports Zone. Future plans here include a sports training centre, a pitch and putt golf centre, outdoor sport fields and hotel development.

Water—if locals aren't skating on its frozen version, they're swimming or fishing in it, sailing on it, or just enjoying its proximity. Photo by Michael Scholz.

Credit River and its tributaries are filled with speckled, rainbow and brown trout; coho, chinook and Atlantic salmon; and small-mouth bass, carp, pickerel and pike. Photo by Michael Scholz.

When you consider that the Indian word *Mississauga* means "river in the north of many mouths", it's no surprise that Mississaugans are drawn to the water. If they're not skating on its frozen version, they're swimming or fishing in it, sailing on it, or just enjoying its proximity. Case in point, the city's version of "On the Waterfront"—the wonderful Mississauga Waterfront Trail.

It provides 15 km of continuous pedestrian and cyclist routes along Lake Ontario, but that's only one reason why the Mississauga Waterfront Trail is so special. Travel its length, and you'll encounter some of the city's most precious and popular landmarks.

Rattray Marsh is a beautiful wetland and the last remaining lakefront marsh between Burlington and Toronto. This environmentally sensitive area, with a self-guided trail, provides a unique habitat for over 700 species of plants, birds, mammals, reptiles and amphibians, and fish.

Lakeside, Meadowland, Meadowood and Jack Darling Parks offer a scenic refuge from the hustle and bustle of city life. Richard's Memorial Park is a gorgeous setting that's popular for wedding photographs, and Rhododendron Gardens showcase rare hybrids and picturesque walkways.

Beyond the well being of citizens, Mississauga's environment benefits from parks, natural areas and an active community. Green spaces and woodlands protect the habitat and watershed systems, and improve air quality. Photo by Michael Scholz.

"At Hershey, we look on our association with the City of Mississauga and involvement with Mississauga's premier sports and entertainment centre as one way to be involved in the community that traditional marketing cannot accomplish. For example, the Hershey Centre's goal of providing the vibrant Mississauga area with countless family events is consistent with the moral fabric in which Hershey operates. Sponsorship of grass roots sports, entertainment and cultural events and properties allows us to reach consumers in unique and effective ways."

Richard W. Meyers
President
Hershey Canada

Opened in 1998, The Hershey Centre is Mississauga's sports and entertainment hub. The 5,400-seat facility, with a capacity of 7,000 for some events, is home to the Mississauga IceDogs of the Ontario Hockey League, featuring the NHL players of tomorrow. Photo by Michael Scholz.

The Bradley Museum is a heritage site that offers a glimpse at life in the 1800s, and the grand Adamson Estate is now home to a division of the Royal Conservatory of Music. The Credit Village Marina and the 40-hectare Lakefront Promenade Park boast of a boardwalk and a play apparatus shaped like—what else?—a giant ship.

That's all great, you can hear the anglers say, but where are the fish biting? Anglers from across Ontario, the border states, and even Europe say that some of the world's best salmon fishing is off of Port Credit, one reason why Mississauga has one of Lake Ontario's largest fleets of charter boats. Credit River and its tributaries are filled with speckled, rainbow and brown trout; coho, chinook and Atlantic salmon; and small-mouth bass, carp, pickerel and pike.

While the City of Mississauga offers its own first-rate recreation facilities and programs, the private and non-profit sectors provide abundant other ways for residents to kick back and re-invigorate themselves. From tennis centres to sports clubs, the choices are endless.

"People here are very active," says Tom Coon, General Manager of the Mississauga YMCA, which has about 10,000 members. Coon says he sees all walks of life, cultures and languages in the "Y." "It's like a little town just here, and that's reflective of the community's participation in recreation."

Playdium, located in the City Centre, is like a little sports town itself. Fans flock to this massive interactive theme park, which also contains a mile-long, Indy-style, go-kart track; a mini-golf course; sand volleyball courts; an outdoor rock-climbing wall; and a baseball centre for pitching and batting practice.

Another major contributor to the local recreation scene is the Mississauga Sports Council. Its mission—encourage residents to be lifelong participants in accessible, safe and equitable sports. Executive Director Blair Webster played minor league hockey himself growing up in Mississauga. He remembers the "life lessons" of sports—teamwork, discipline, self-esteem and leadership. Today, he's delighted to see how Mississaugans have the chance to participate in such healthy pursuits, in all senses of the word.

"Mississauga has excellent opportunities for all types of sports," says Webster. "To me, we're right up there with the best of any other city in the country."

For children, recreation develops motor and social skills. For youth, it's a positive lifestyle choice and provides a healthy framework for interaction with adults. Photo by Michael Scholz.

"Any city that's held up as a healthy community must have lots of opportunities for people to participate in leisure activities," said Tom Coon, General Manager of the Mississauga YMCA. Photo by Michael Scholz.

Recreation also provides some of the best opportunities for Mississaugans to become volunteers. The city's recreation infrastructure, from program organizers to coaches to officials, couldn't survive without its enthusiastic volunteers. Coon says that being engaged as a volunteer can offer the same benefits as active play—"You're healthier, happier, and live longer," he says.

Beyond the well being of citizens, Mississauga's environment benefits from parks, natural areas and an active community. Green spaces and woodlands protect the habitat and watershed systems, and improve air quality. Trails and paths encourage walking and cycling instead of driving. "Outdoor recreation creates an awareness of environmental issues," says Mitcham.

It's no stretch to say that strong recreation and a strong city—economically, physically, environmentally and socially—are linked.

"Any city that's held up as a healthy community must have lots of opportunities for people to participate in leisure activities," says Coon. "Mississauga has done a great job of providing a network of recreation programs and parks, encouraging participation, and making it accessible."❖

Recreation isn't just fun and games. There are serious benefits for both individuals and the community. Look at how activity reduces stress and the risk of illness.

"Even a one per cent increase in the participation rate in physical activity in Mississauga would save about $300 million a year in health care costs," says Webster, citing a government study.

A strong recreation infrastructure and an active population help Mississauga in many other ways, says Mitcham. For children, recreation develops motor and social skills. For youth, it's a positive lifestyle choice and provides a healthy framework for interaction with adults. For seniors, it helps maintain independence and an involvement in community life. For people with disabilities, it can be a route to social interaction and a way to acquire life skills. And for anyone at any stage, recreation offers an outlet to develop his or her physical, social, creative and intellectual potential.

While the city's extensive leisure options improve the quality of life for individual residents of Mississauga, Mitcham says sports, parks and recreation also contribute to community building.

For instance, by drawing broad participation from across society, recreation builds understanding among residents and connects communities. The state of local recreation and teams also creates a sense of community pride. And recreation opportunities and green spaces increase property values, making Mississauga more appealing to visitors and attracting business, an economic catalyst for the entire city.

Mississauga gives a nod of approbation to recreation and athletics. As an illustration, the city contains 311 soccer fields and 273 baseball diamonds for athletes of all ages and levels. Pictured here is the Mississauga Majors, whose goal is "to foster, promote and teach its members to play amateur baseball to the best of their abilities and to provide the maximum opportunity and best possible environment for all eligible members." Photo below and opposite courtesy of the Mississauga Majors.

Chapter Six

THAT'S ENTERTAINMENT

Mississauga boasts an incredible range of cultural options, from galleries to the theatre, concerts to clubs, where people can turn to stimulate, entertain and enthrall themselves. Photo by Michael Scholz.

To Daniel Donaldson, CEO of Mississauga's Living Arts Centre, few things define a city's sophistication more than its artistic and cultural climate. "A strong arts infrastructure," says Donaldson, "is a testament to the maturity of any community."

If that's the case, then Mississauga has reached a critical phase in its development. For the city boasts an incredible range of cultural options, from galleries to the theatre, concerts to clubs, where people here can turn to stimulate, entertain and enthrall themselves.

"When you have a strong cultural base, your city becomes more worldly," says Dominic Hay, President of the Mississauga Arts Council. "The arts lift the spirit of the community."

The most visible expression of the city's artistic emergence is the Living Arts Centre, which opened in 1997. Not only the top venue for arts in the city, the 210,000-square-foot LAC is one of the premiere cultural complexes in the country.

Located just north of the Mississauga Civic Centre, the LAC was designed as a versatile focal point for the arts in Mississauga. It features two theatres—the 1,300-seat Hammerson Hall, with the highest possible acoustic rating for a concert venue, and the 400-seat Royal Bank Theatre, as well as exhibit spaces for visual artists.

Just about any type of production imaginable can and has been performed at the LAC. This is the home to the nationally acclaimed Mississauga Symphony, the Mississauga Choral Society, and Opera Mississauga, three of the city's cultural touchstones.

But the LAC is so much more. This is a place where you can hear a Bach concerto one night, and see a circus the next. A night of Broadway showstoppers, the *Nutcracker* ballet, a jazz combo, award-winning dramas, swing bands, musical comedies, the opera *Carmen*, children's entertainers, acrobats, pop groups—all are equally at home on the LAC stage.

This isn't just a home for professionals; the LAC encourages Mississauga's artists of tomorrow by offering students courses in pottery, photography, painting and drawing, dance, textiles, home decoration, glass-blowing, wood working, drama and songwriting.

As one local schoolteacher notes, the LAC serves as "a heart to the arts," and a reminder of how highly the arts are valued and promoted in Mississauga.

"The fact that the city built this facility was a bold and impressive statement," says Donaldson. "I can't think of another venue in Canada that combines the performing and visual arts under one roof like this, and also offers the business world a unique venue for meetings and seminars."

In the world of dance, Mississauga kicks up its feet with troupes that include the Mississauga Ballet Company, Longlade Dance Company and the Grant School of Irish Dancing. Photo by Michael Scholz.

*The Mississauga Players, the Mississauga Youth Theatre, and Music Theatre
Mississauga are only some of the leading lights on the theatre scene.
Photo by Michael Scholz.*

܀ঌৡৣঌ

While the LAC is a tangible sign of the city's cultural rise, Mississauga has had a long tradition of excellence in the arts. For instance, just the city's vocal and instrumental groups alone showcase an astonishing array of talent. Apart from the Mississauga Symphony, Mississauga Choral Society, and Opera Mississauga, there is the Mississauga Festival Choir, Mississauga Children's Choir, Mississauga "Pops" Concert Band, Mississauga Big Band Jazz Ensemble, Mississauga Youth Orchestra, Emerald Knights Drum and Bugle Corps, and the Sinfonia Mississauga chamber orchestra. If there were a soundtrack to the city, Mississauga would sure have an eclectic and melodious mix.

In the world of dance, Mississauga kicks up its feet with troupes that include the Mississauga Ballet Company, Longlade Dance Company and the Grant School of Irish Dancing.

Mississauga can also draw the curtains on energetic theatre. There is the 400-seat Meadowvale Theatre, which was the city's number one venue until the LAC came along, and Harbourside Playhouse in Port Credit, one of Ontario's fastest growing theatres. Mississauga also has a lively dinner theatre, Stage West, featuring well-known performers in comedy/musical favourites.

The Mississauga Players, the Mississauga Youth Theatre, and Music Theatre Mississauga are only some of the leading lights on the theatre scene. The city's community theatres, about a dozen strong, give residents a chance to not only enjoy fine plays as members of the audience, but to take centre stage themselves as performers.

In the visual arts, the 3,500-square-foot Art Gallery of Mississauga is a champion of homegrown artists. The emphasis is on Canadian art, with over half of the works exhibited by locals. The location in the high-traffic Mississauga Civic Centre gives the public gallery valuable exposure. Here, citizens of Mississauga don't have to experience the arts as works that just hang on a gallery wall; members of the public can rent and, if desired, buy the inspired artwork.

"We're here to educate the public about art, which can capture the history and culture of Mississauga, and bring a broad brush of exhibitions to the community," says Fred Troughton, Executive Director, Art Gallery of Mississauga.

Another major public gallery, the Blackwood, opened in 1969 as the Erindale College Art Gallery, the first gallery in the entire region. Today, its exhibitions focus on Canadian contemporary artists. In the

"When you have a strong cultural base, your city becomes more worldly," says Dominic Hay, President of the Mississauga Arts Council. *"The arts lift the spirit of the community."* Photo by Michael Scholz.

Mississauga has many troupes that proudly express their unique heritage, from the Barvinok Ukrainian Folk Dancing School to the Himig Filipino Choral Ensemble and many others. Photo by Michael Scholz.

⁊⁊⁊⁊⁊

spring, Blackwood Gallery showcases the work of Erindale College and Sheridan College art students, and in the summer they hold children's art classes.

While a city's arts scene is identified with its major arts venues, that's not the whole story in Mississauga. At the grass-roots level, there are dozens of smaller art societies, crafts guilds (from quilting to ceramics), literary clubs, and hundreds of classes in every form of the arts, letting residents tap into their creative side.

Not surprising for such an ethnically varied community, Mississauga also has many troupes that proudly express their unique heritage, from the Barvinok Ukrainian Folk Dancing School to the Himig Filipino Choral Ensemble. Now *that's* cultural diversity!

And like any other big city, Mississauga has a wide range of clubs that feature everything from dancing to comedy to live bands, contributing to an active and varied nightlife.

Says Daniel Donaldson, CEO of Mississauga's Living Arts Centre, "I can't think of another venue in Canada that combines the performing and visual arts under one roof like this, and also offers the business world a unique venue for meetings and seminars." Photo by Michael Scholz.

The most visible expression of Mississauga's artistic emergence is the Living Arts Centre. Since its opening in 1997, the 210,000-square-foot LAC has been not only the top venue for arts in the city, but one of the premiere cultural complexes in the country as well. Photo by Michael Scholz.

The surge of interest in the arts in Mississauga is like a snowball rolling down a hill. It keeps growing and growing, building on itself.

You can sense that the growing passion for and allure of the arts is widespread. There are the tens of thousands of members of arts audiences—the theatre and concert-goers and gallery visitors. There are the thousands of residents who actively participate in the arts—as artists themselves, whether amateur or performers, and as members of arts organizations. And there are the hundreds of businesses who support the arts—as sponsors of arts groups and performances.

There is also an indispensable local resource—the Mississauga Arts Council. Created by the city in 1981, the council is the only organization in Mississauga that represents all art disciplines and interests. Its mandate—to foster and promote artistic expression and appreciation for the arts.

This umbrella organization, which includes over 170 arts groups and 1,000 individual members, offers operating grants, participates in arts festivals and events, is involved in government relations, and holds the annual Mississauga Arts Awards. To the art council's Hay, a sculptor by trade, Mississauga has grown by leaps and bounds artistically.

The Living Arts Center isn't just a venue for professional artistic expression; it encourages the artists of tomorrow by offering students courses in pottery, photography, painting and drawing, dance, textiles, home decoration, glass-blowing, wood working, drama and songwriting. Photos by Michael Scholz.

"We're young here, as a city and demographically, and that brings a certain vibrancy and energy to the arts," says Hay. "We're at an exciting phase of developing our permanent arts institutions and striking our own identity."

Hay has an interesting theory on the range of advantages that a strong cultural community gives to a city. Aside from the usual benefits—a chance for people to express and enjoy works of art, and the economic spin-offs from strong cultural industries—Hay sees a plus for local businesses. And not just because the arts scene makes the city more livable for its employees. "The presence of the arts helps establish a creative ethos in the community," says Hay. "Our residents become more creative people, and bring that creative thinking into the workplace too."

Photo by Michael Scholz.

(Left) The Living Arts Center is the home of the nationally acclaimed Mississauga Symphony, the Mississauga Choral Society, and Opera Mississauga, three of the city's cultural touchstones. Photo by Michael Scholz.

The Springbank Arts Centre, operated by Visual Arts Mississauga, is a non-profit charitable organization that encourages artistic expression. It is open to everyone for classes, workshops, group meetings, children's art camps, fine art exhibitions, and craft sales throughout the year. Photo by Michael Scholz.

Mississauga's enthusiasm for the arts is manifest in the number of local arts festivals held outdoors in the spring, summer, and fall. Photo by Michael Scholz.

Add that to the long list of what the arts achieve for Mississauga. Ultimately, says Donaldson, "The arts is a form of beauty, and that's just important to have in your life."

Chris Giacinti, Manager of the Meadowvale Theatre, echoes that sentiment. "A community is more than just the place *where* we live; it defines *how* we live, in the opportunities for us to explore and experience life and share those experiences. Where athletics contribute to our physical well being, the arts nurture our emotional health. Together, they make our community come alive."❖

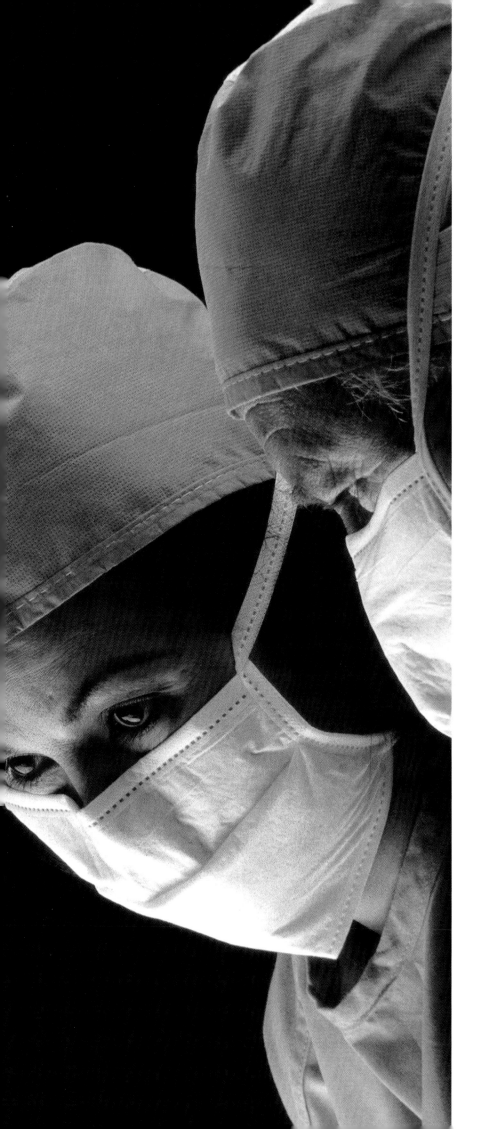

Mississauga's community of healthcare facilities is a top-ranked network of innovative hospitals, community programs that help residents prevent illness, and a flourishing local pharmaceutical sector that's discovering new ways to treat and prevent diseases. Photo by Don Wolf

⤷ↂↃↄ⤶

You can evaluate a city's health in many ways, from its growth rate to its ability to attract investment. But another measure of a healthy community is, literally, its physical health. What kind of shape are area residents, and area health care services, in?

By that standard, Mississauga is thriving. A *Maclean's* magazine survey of the best health care in Canada ranked the Mississauga region second. Take the pulse of wellness in Mississauga, and you find innovative hospitals, community programs that help residents prevent illness, and a flourishing local pharmaceutical sector that's discovering new ways to treat and prevent diseases.

"Mississauga," says Michael Cloutier, President of Pharmacia Canada, "has successfully embraced both the private and public health-care sectors."

The city's health-care providers aim high. Enter the lobby of Credit Valley Hospital ("a light and airy lobby designed to put patients at ease," says *Maclean's*), and you're met by a giant poster that proclaims the CVH vision—"to be the finest hospital in Canada".

"We constantly look at the way we do things, and try to find ways of doing them better," says Wayne Fyffe, the hospital's CEO.

The 366-bed CVH is more than a community hospital. It operates the regional genetic screening and kidney dialysis programs and, after a five-year, $200 million expansion, will become a regional centre for cancer and pediatrics. The expansion is also giving CVH a new wing of beds, meeting the rapid growth in northwest Mississauga.

CVH is known for its caring environment—"competency and compassion," as a patient wrote in a thank you letter. That attitude extends to community outreach. One example is an asthma education program offered in schools that takes the mystery out of asthma for the kids and helps teachers recognize the warning signs of an asthma episode. Through another public education series, CVH health professionals share information on everything from stress to body image.

Both CVH and Mississauga's other community hospital, Trillium Health Centre, have received awards by the Canadian Council on Health Facilities Accreditation, recognizing their excellence in health care. The two hospitals also share a standing as key regional health facilities.

Trillium (with one site in Mississauga and one in nearby Etobicoke) is one of Ontario's largest community hospitals, with some 700 beds. Along with delivering primary and secondary health care, Trillium is the regional centre for neurosurgery, advanced cardiac services, and complex musculoskeletal services. In a joint venture with Extendicare Canada, Trillium also operates a chronic care facility and over 100 interim long-term care beds at the Queensway site.

The addition of the comprehensive cardiac program was especially notable—Ontario's first to open in 10 years, and only the second outside of a teaching hospital. The program will handle 3,300 cardiac catheterizations, 1,100 cardiac surgeries and 800 angioplasties annually, about 10 per cent of all such procedures in Ontario.

"Advanced cardiac services at Trillium will be of tremendous benefit our community," says Wendy Nelson, Vice-President of Patient Services. "People needing sophisticated cardiac tests, procedures and heart surgery can receive the best care much closer to home than ever before."

As effective as they are, Trillium and CVH are only part of a broad system of ensuring superior health care in Mississauga. The Community Care Access

Both Credit Valley Hospital and Mississauga's other community hospital, Trillium Health Centre, have received awards by the Canadian Council on Health Facilities Accreditation, recognizing their excellence in health care. The two hospitals also share a standing as key regional health facilities.
Photo by Bill Bachmann

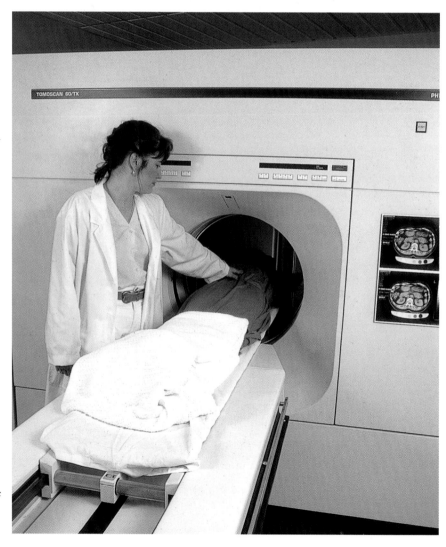

Centre (CCAC) for Peel Region is another important resource. This agency gives residents a single point of access to information on over 700 community health and social service organizations in Mississauga and the region.

The CCAC team works closely with clients, family members, caregivers, and service agencies to facilitate everything from in-home physiotherapy to speech language programs for children in the schools. Services are aimed at preventing hospital admissions or decreasing the length of hospital stays, enabling people to remain in their homes. If that's no longer possible, the CCAC helps coordinate placement to a long-term care facility.

Another partner in improving community health is the Peel Health Department. Its mandate is broad. One division promotes healthy lifestyles—proper eating, activity, no smoking or substance abuse, and injury prevention. Another ensures environmental health—safe food and drinks in restaurants and processing plants, and water quality in pools, wells and sewage systems. Yet another division protects the public from

reportable and sexually transmitted diseases—an immunization program, and counseling and clinical services related to birth control and HIV/AIDS. And still another division promotes family health—positive pregnancies and early intervention programs that improve the developmental prospects for young children.

While Peel Health programs reach thousands of residents in person, support is just a phone call away; the Health Line Peel handles over 60,000 calls a year, offering easy access to extensive and essential health-care advice.

A spirit of partnership exemplifies health care in Mississauga. Look at the Next Step to Active Living, a rehabilitation program for people who were recently released from the hospital. It occurs at a Mississauga community centre, a joint effort of CVH, the CCAC, and the city's Recreation and Parks Division—a telling example of community cooperation towards a common objective.

A Maclean's *magazine survey of the best health care in Canada ranked the Mississauga region second. Photo by Michael Rush.*

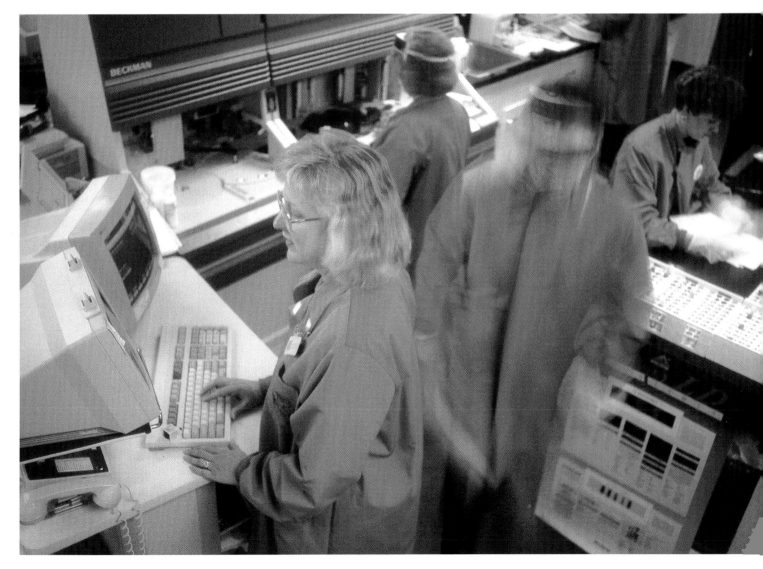

"By working together, we have better physical and social outcomes," says Cathy Szabo, CEO of the CCAC. "The goal is to provide the appropriate care in the appropriate place, to keep people as well as possible—and being well also means feeling part of the community."

In creating an environment that promotes the pursuit of health-care excellence, Mississauga has another advantage—the local presence of many of the world's top pharmaceutical companies. The benefits, to the people of Mississauga and to all Canadians, are far-reaching.

For one, the pharmaceutical multinationals who make Mississauga their Canadian home spend hundreds of millions of dollars a year between them on research and development in this country. The medical advances have been astonishing. New treatments for AIDS, arthritis, asthma, cancer, cardiovascular disease, epilepsy, osteoporosis, pain control, and much more—all are related to the clinical and basic research carried out or funded by Mississauga's pharmaceutical companies.

In creating an environment that promotes the pursuit of healthcare excellence, Mississauga has another advantage—the local presence of many of the world's top pharmaceutical companies. Photo by Michael Rush.

These firms are mindful of Mississauga's strength as a health care centre. AstraZeneca, GlaxoSmithKline, Merck Frosst and Pharmacia have all been major backers of the Applied Biosciences and Biotechnology program at the University of Toronto at Mississauga (UTM). That includes scholarships to encourage the community's health-care leaders of tomorrow.

Supporting UTM, says GlaxoSmithKline CEO Paul Lucas, "enhances Mississauga's position as a focal point for biotechnology and training."

While the local university is a natural target for the pharmaceutical firms' generosity, it is hardly the only recipient. GlaxoSmithKline has established a fund to create research positions in every medical school in the country. The firm has also given millions of dollars worth of goods to Mississauga-based MAP International of Canada, which does humanitarian medical work around the world.

For its part, Merck Frosst founded the Alliance for Science Education Enrichment. This network of industry, education and government agencies works to increase the comfort level of elementary school teachers in teaching science, technology and math. Through the Alliance, Merck Frosst has

The city's pharmaceutical firms, hospitals, university science programs, regional health department and Community Care Access Centre, and other agencies draws thousands of world-class doctors, researchers and other health-care experts to Mississauga. Photo by JoAnne Frederick.

in Mississauga. As Lucas said at the time: "It's about finding new ways to help people when they're sick or in pain. It's about healing. It's about saving lives."

Those sentiments guide Mississauga's entire health-care community. The pharmaceutical firms, hospitals, university science programs, active regional health department and CCAC, and other agencies have all created a critical mass—one that draws thousands of world-class doctors, researchers and other health-care experts to the city. "The best and the brightest," as Fyffe calls them. No wonder that Mississauga is one of the country's healthiest communities.

"We enjoy some of the best quality of care in Canada," says Dr. Joseph Wong, a surgeon at Credit Valley Hospital, and co-chair of a capital campaign to build the Yee Hong geriatric centre in Mississauga. "People here work from the heart to make the health-care system work."❖

Mississauga-based pharmaceutical firms give high praise for how the local government understands just what the sector brings to Mississauga in high-quality jobs and in cutting edge health care solutions. The relationship between the city and its healthcare industries ensures a bright future for the local medical community. Photo by Michael Rush.

sent many of its scientists into classrooms and created a science education resource centre, helping to spark interest in careers in science and health care.

AstraZeneca Canada is another firm that takes its community responsibility seriously. The company, which has been in Mississauga since 1961, is an enthusiastic supporter of local causes, from health-related groups like the Mississauga chapter of the Canadian Cancer Society, to civic events like Canada Day celebrations.

The pharmaceutical firms give high praise for how the local government understands just what the sector brings to Mississauga, in high-quality jobs and in cutting edge health care solutions. "There is no better place to do business," says Cloutier.

Sheila Frame, Vice-President of Corporate Affairs, at AstraZeneca, recalls how a few years ago, "The Mayor personally jumped on a plane to Sweden to argue why our parent company should make an investment in Mississauga—and they did."

GlaxoSmithKline made a significant investment of its own in 1997, a $120 million technical centre

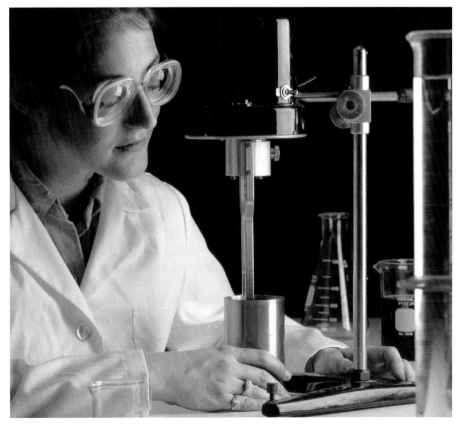

Chapter Eight

SCHOOL OF THOUGHT

Mississauga benefits from the quality and variety of education available locally at all levels from early childhood education all the way through college. Photo by Michael Scholz.

In 1834 King William IV granted 200 acres of land, "for the encouragement of learning among our loving subjects" in the land that would become Mississauga. School life was different then. Besides the "three R's," the schoolmaster or schoolmistress taught bible verses, physiology and temperance. Girls wore dresses with a petticoat, pinafore and stockings; boys dressed in knickerbockers with knee-length socks, suspenders, and a shirt and tie. Attendance only became compulsory in 1871, for children 7-12 years, for at least four months of the year.

Education has evolved greatly since then. While "the encouragement of learning has always been important" in Mississauga. From public schools to university programs to vocational training, the city has one of Canada's most progressive educational environments.

"Mississauga is well served by the quality and variety of education here," says Robert McNutt, Principal of the University of Toronto at Mississauga (UTM).

"We're committed to survive and thrive as a learning community," adds Harold Brathwaite, Chair of the Peel District School Board (PDSB).

Photo by Bill Bachmann.

The Peel District School Board believes in setting high expectations for students, giving them an equal opportunity to develop their full potential, and creating the foundation to succeed in learning at every stage in life. Photo by Bill Bachmann.

Start with the PDSB, one of Canada's largest public school boards, serving 107,000 students in 184 schools (60 per cent of them in Mississauga). Through its Centre for Education and Training, the board also serves 300,000 adult and part-time learners. In fact, this centre is Canada's largest provider of workplace training.

Teaching students to be lifelong learners—that's part of the PDSB mission. The board believes in setting high expectations for students, giving them an equal opportunity to develop their full potential, and creating the foundation to succeed in learning at every stage in life.

These are challenges that any school board faces, but by several measures, PDSB is doing better than most. Consider the tests conducted by the Education Quality and Accountability Office, where PDSB students consistently perform better than the provincial average, or look at a survey of PDSB parents, who give the board high marks for teacher planning, assessment of student progress, and positive student behaviour.

A report by the Education Improvement Commission, a government body, cited a dozen areas of effective PDSB practices that other boards can emulate. These ranged from establishing community partnerships, to developing action plans for system-wide success.

"If this was a report card, we got an A," says Brathwaite. "I've always known this board does an exceptional job. But it's reassuring to have an outside group confirm that. The review team found a clear sense of pride in the quality of education in Peel schools."

That quality extends to the Dufferin-Peel Catholic District School Board, which operates 120 schools that serve 82,000 students, just over 60 per cent of those in Mississauga. Catholic education is an integral part of Ontario's publicly funded education system. In fact, the Dufferin-Peel Board is among the fastest growing school boards in the province and has embarked on an aggressive capital building program to accommodate increased enrollment.

Tests conducted by the Education Quality and Accountability Office show that Peel District School Board students consistently perform better than the provincial average. Photo by Wally Emerson.

On top of the standard provincial curriculum, the Dufferin-Peel Board offers strong religious and family life education. To Michael Bator, Director of Education, a Catholic education "imparts a tradition of caring and compassion, and a record of excellence and achievement."

"Catholic education necessarily and naturally engages students, parents and teachers in the learning enterprise, one which respects and cherishes the whole person as one of dignity, hope and promise," says Bator.

Both the Dufferin-Peel Board and the PDSB have an impressive lineup of co-op, French, and special education programs to meet each student's individual needs. The two boards also work together to benefit students and staff. Cooperative ventures include a reading recovery program for "at risk" students, speech therapy programs, and summer institutes for teachers.

Beyond the public and Catholic school boards, Mississauga has dozens of private schools that offer everything from alternative education to technical and vocational skills.

At the post-secondary level, the city is home to the University of Toronto at Mississauga, which offers a wide range of programs in the humanities,

Peel District School Board is one of Canada's largest public school boards, and serves 107,000 students in 184 schools (60 per cent of them in Mississauga). Photo by Bill Bachmann.

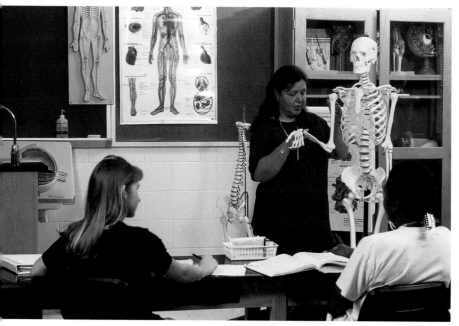

From public schools to university programs to vocational training, Mississauga has one of Canada's most progressive educational environments. Photo by Bill Bachmann.

UTM students and faculty, in turn, are highly involved in the community, mounting everything from food drives to cancer fundraisers. McNutt himself has chaired the local United Way campaign. And the UTM calendar is filled with public lectures and business forums, art gallery events and theatre productions, science fairs and arts camps—enlightening area residents, and enhancing the school's impact on life in Mississauga.

"The university has lots to offer Mississauga, not least of which is our graduates," McNutt says. "We're an important part of the economic life of the city."

Beyond the public and Catholic school boards, Mississauga has dozens of private schools that offer everything from alternative education to technical and vocational skills. Photo by Bill Bachmann.

social sciences, sciences and management, and has two Masters programs, in Management and Professional Accounting and Biotechnology.

Part of the University of Toronto, one of North America's most respected academic and research institutions, UTM has attracted an outstanding teaching staff. In fact, UTM professors have received more Ontario Confederation of University Faculty Associations awards, the province's top teaching honour, than professors at any other University of Toronto college or faculty.

UTM is experiencing its greatest growth since being formed as Erindale College in 1976. About 6,400 graduate and undergraduate students attend UTM, and that's expected to grow to 10,000. McNutt says UTM students benefit from a continually upgraded curriculum, an enthusiastic faculty that's involved in world-class research, and a "caring" environment—all amidst a scenic 224-acre campus on the banks of the Credit River.

"We believe," says McNutt, "that a University of Toronto degree earned at its Mississauga campus is an unbeatable combination."

The university and Mississauga communities have long been mutually supportive. In recent years, for instance, several local pharmaceutical companies were among the biggest financial donors to a new Centre for Applied Biosciences and Biotechnology. The City of Mississauga itself was the first to throw its support behind plans for an innovative School of Communication, Culture and Information Technology.

Mississaugans have close access to the greatest concentration of post-secondary institutions in Canada. Almost 20 universities and colleges lie within an 80 km radius. Photo by Wally Emerson.

UTM aside, Mississaugans have close access to the greatest concentration of post-secondary institutions in Canada. Almost 20 universities and colleges lie within an 80 km radius. The universities include McMaster (Hamilton); Waterloo and Wilfrid Laurier (Waterloo); Guelph (Guelph); Toronto, Ryerson Polytechnical and York (Toronto); and Brock (St. Catharine's). Colleges include Sheridan (Brampton and Oakville); Centennial, George Brown, Humber, Seneca and the Ontario College of Art and Design (Toronto); Durham (Oshawa); Conestoga (Kitchener); Mohawk (Hamilton); and Niagara (Welland).

Back in town, Mississauga residents and employees can also take advantage of terrific business-related education at the Richard Ivey School of Business Executive Development Centre, and at the DeVry Institute of Technology, focusing on electronics and computers.

Learning opportunities aren't just found in schools. Part of being a well-educated community is access to public libraries; Mississauga has 13, strategically located throughout the city. The Central Library, part of the Civic Centre, is Canada's busiest central library. It houses 250,000 books, extensive audio-visual media, global data-bases, and a Career Resource Centre.

Another vital part of education is an understanding of your community's history. Two local museums help convey that heritage—the Bradley Museum, which emphasizes the lives of 19th century settlers, and the Benares farmhouse, which has been restored to the 1918 period. The Britannia Schoolhouse, built in 1852, was restored to appear as it did in the 1920s and 1930s— today's students can spend a day in the classroom and learn what school was like "way back when."

The high quality of education in Mississauga, all through the years and in all its forms, is one reason why the people of this city are positioned to meet the challenges of the 21st century, as members of the workforce and simply as citizens.

Brathwaite talks about how developing a creative, motivated and well-qualified work force begins with what people experience in childhood. To succeed at work or life, people must draw upon a wide assortment of skills— things like problem solving, adaptability, teamwork and communication.

"Have you ever considered where people learn these important skills? It begins in childhood," says Brathwaite. "The terms we use in education may be different—learning readiness, secure attachments, physical well-being, social engagement, smart risk-taking—but the essence is the same."

"A positive childhood combined with student success can pave the way to a prosperous future," he continues. "Ultimately, students who are blessed with this strong foundation will play an important role in the world we live in."

Mississauga's educators have proven their skill at laying this foundation— a foundation upon which is being built a more dynamic Mississauga.❖

One of North America's most respected academic and research institutions, the University of Toronto at Mississauga offers a wide range of programs in the humanities, social sciences, sciences and management, and has two Masters programs, in Management and Professional Accounting and Biotechnology. Photo by Michael Scholz.

PARTNERS IN PROGRESS

Photo by Michael Scholz

Chapter Nine

❖

BUSINESS, FINANCE & DEVELOPMENT

Photo by Michael Scholz

Mississauga Board of Trade

*E*ven the largest maple tree starts from a seed. It grows, adds branches as it matures and, eventually, reaches a majestic height with a trunk so thick that a man can't wrap his arms around it.

The growth of the Mississauga Board of Trade (MBOT) is similar.

MBOT, a private sector, non-profit, volunteer-driven business organization funded mainly by membership fees, has more than 1,300 member companies, representing 65,000 employees—more than 10 per cent of the city's entire corporate population.

The board started in 1976 as the seed of an idea in the minds of a small group of visionary local business leaders who saw the need for an organization to represent the many businesses that were taking root in what is now known as the City of Mississauga.

The mission of the Mississauga Board of Trade "is to create an environment for Mississauga business to compete and prosper, in recognition of the simple truth that a thriving business sector contributes to the quality of life for all citizens in our community."

The board's mandate is to be the "Network for Success" of business in Mississauga on all issues of concern to the Mississauga business community. The board has three core 'businesses': lobbying, networking and providing an extensive list of member services.

Hundreds of dedicated volunteers act to fulfill that mandate. "We have been fortunate over the years to have the top business leaders in the city participate actively in the board, serving on committees, at the director and executive levels and as president. Our 'wall of fame'—pictures of former presidents—is a who's who of business in Mississauga," Managing Director David Gordon says.

The Board's new home Riverwood, the former Chappell Estate on Burnhamthorpe Road, overlooks the Credit River and was once home to one of Mississauga's most influential businessmen.

A special award of excellence was given to Mayor Hazel McCallion on the occasion of the Board's 25th anniversary.

"Fortunately, many of our former presidents have retained their ties to the board by serving on the Board of Governors, a group that we occasionally call upon for advice on issues of significance to our membership."

As one of the top boards of trade in Canada, the MBOT wields significant influence at all levels of government. Municipally, the board has forged a strong, mutually beneficial working relationship with Mississauga mayor Hazel McCallion and her council, as well as city staff. At the regional level, the board provides a strong, reasonable voice on issues of concern to all businesses and residents in Peel.

Provincially, the board has the ear of the many local members of provincial parliament; federally, the city's members look to the board for guidance and leadership. It is little wonder that local MP Steve Mahoney is the chair of the Ontario caucus for the ruling liberal government.

When free trade among Canada, the United States and Mexico was an issue in the early 1990s, the MBOT was there, organizing special seminars and meetings to make members aware of what the North American Free Trade Agreement would mean to them. Later, the board played a leadership role with the MERCOSUR countries, a trade bloc comprised of Argentina, Brazil, Uruguay and Paraguay.

While the City of Mississauga continues to grow at a breathtaking rate—construction starts exceeded $1 billion for three consecutive years—the Mississauga Board of Trade has also become a major force in the Canadian chamber movement. Its influence is felt right up to the prime ministerial level, where Jean Chretien honored the MBOT recently by making a special trip to the city to honor a commitment he'd made two years previously.

"There is strength in numbers," Gordon says. "We possess the size and reputation to advocate effectively on behalf of our member companies on everything from taxes to labor legislation. We know who our audience is and what it needs and wants from us, and we have the staff and core of volunteer experts necessary to produce results."

Board of Directors with the honourable Jean Cretien, prime minister of Canada.

While the board can deliver on its promise to influence people and affect decisions, it also provides an excellent opportunity for members and their guests to network at both business and social events. The MBOT's many committees offer numerous opportunities for members to not only share ideas and knowledge but also to do business.

One area where the Mississauga Board of Trade's size and influence really come into play is in the Board's ability to provide its members with a wide array of services—everything from extended health care to low-cost cellular and long-distance telephone plans, home and auto insurance, notarization of certificates of origin for export shipments and special credit card merchant rates.

Like the maple tree that has to be transplanted when it gets too big, the MBOT has outgrown its long-time location at the heart of the city across from Square One and has moved to the former Chappell Estate on Burnhamthorpe Road, west of Creditview. This historic property, overlooking the Credit River, was once home to one of Mississauga's most influential businessmen.

"It's fitting that the board selected this property as its new home," says Gordon, "because it represents the best of what the area had to offer more than 75 years ago but retains all its charm. It's going to be a wonderful home for the board for many years to come."❖

Board of Directors with Ontario Premier Mike Harris.

Orlando Corporation

Orlando Corporation, headquartered in Mississauga, is one of Canada's largest privately owned real estate development companies. Established more than 70 years ago, the company specializes in the design, development and management of all types of industrial, office and retail properties.

Orlando offers clients a total package of vertically integrated real estate development services including: project evaluation, site selection, architectural and engineering design, construction, financing, leasing and property management.

Almost every citizen in Mississauga either works in or passes by an Orlando building every day, since it has designed and constructed office, industrial and retail complexes for most of the major companies in the city. Some of the more familiar names include Subaru Canada, Michelin Canada, Canadian Red Cross Society, Microsoft, Oracle, Pepsi Canada, Revenue Canada, Fuji Photo Canada, Home Depot, Costco, Xerox, Ingram Micro and the Royal Bank.

The Heartland Town Centre, a retail power centre at Britannia and Mavis Roads also owned by Orlando, has been the model for all such centres now common throughout the Greater Toronto Area.

Orlando's team of in-house professionals, guided by a commitment to excellence, has designed and developed more than 60 million square feet of industrial, office and retail properties. The portfolio of properties owned and managed by the company exceeds 32 million square feet. Stable rental income, combined with prudent asset management, provides Orlando with a reliable foundation from which to fund current operating requirements and future expansion.

Ingram Micro, 55 Standish Court, Mississauga.

Orlando Corporation, 6205 Airport Road, Mississauga.

Orlando's seven master-planned business parks—from Mississauga in the west to Scarborough in the east—spread across the Greater Toronto Area, providing clients with an excellent choice of sites where Orlando designs and builds accommodation for sale or lease. In addition, Orlando can either design and build on land owned by the client, or find a site better suited to a client's needs.

"Orlando has the best land holdings in Mississauga and the best design staff to develop them," Phil King, senior vice-president, development, and a long time member of the MBOT Executive, says proudly.

Clients who select Orlando's total design/build concept are assured of accommodation that is as unique as their business profile. They can always depend on Orlando to take full responsibility for all phases of the construction process including: site selection, regulatory approvals, architectural and engineering design, space planning, interior layout, building technologies and building operating deficiencies. Since all of its services are performed in-house, Orlando is able to offer clients firm delivery dates, stipulated price contracts and fixed lease rates.

Orlando's construction division is known and respected in the industry as a leader and innovator. The dedicated team of construction experts, many of whom have been with the company for several decades or more, use tried, tested and proven building practices, enhanced by the advanced application of today's information and technology tools.

"Orlando believes very strongly in life-cycle leasing, whereby buildings are not necessarily designed solely for the current tenant. We're looking 15 or more years down the road to the next tenant. Our buildings have a very long shelf life; they're as attractive and functional 20 years after construction as they are the first day they're occupied," says King. That philosophy doesn't go

RCA, 6200 Edwards Boulevard, Mississauga.

unnoticed; Orlando has one of the highest tenant retention ratios and lowest overall vacancy rates in the industry.

Orlando provides the largest inventory of industrial space in Canada. "When new space is not required, virtually every size and type of building becomes available for our clients' requirements through our life cycle program."

"We are financially secure and we continue to grow every year. We have a good blend of young and older staff with their corresponding range of experience. Orlando's own head office complex, on Airport Road near Terminal 3, has existed for almost 40 years. "We're part of this community, and we intend to remain as such," says King.

"Doug Kilner, Orlando's president for the past 22 years, was a Credit Valley Hospital Board of Governor for 12 years and chairman for 3. Also, Orlando's Chairman Carlo Fidani has recently made a significant financial contribution to the Credit Valley Hospital, showing his support not only for health care, but for the specific community in which we work."

There is additional growth potential of unserviced land in the Mississauga area, and much of it has been acquired by Orlando as well. A 500-acre site is located at Highway #407 and Mississauga Road, on the Mississauga-Brampton boundary. It's called the Churchill Business Community and will be developed over the next few years,

beginning mid-2001. "It's one of the last remaining parcels of developable land assembled in the area," says King.

Pave-Al Limited, Orlando's road building division, serves the company's project needs as well as undertaking road building works for the province, local municipalities and other developers. Pave-Al provides timely and cost-effective solutions for a diverse range of projects including: the construction and refurbishing of bridge and underpass structures, municipal underground services, highways and municipal roads. Asphalt materials for these projects, as well as other consumers, originate at the company's manufacturing plant located in Mississauga.

Orlando's property management division provides a comprehensive package of services, each designed to contribute to the comfort and well being of its tenants. Properties within its portfolio are inspected regularly to ensure that each meets the company's strict environmental and maintenance standards. All buildings receive on-site service by a team of committed professionals.

"The mayor and city council have done an outstanding job of helping us in attracting new business to Mississauga," says King. But in the end, it's up to companies such as Orlando that ensure they stay and prosper by providing appropriate and well maintained facilities. We achieve our success through their success; it's a win-win situation."

Orlando Corporation certainly is a winner—in every sense of the word. ❖

Nippon Express, 6250 Edwards Boulevard, Mississauga.

Kelly Services (Canada) Ltd.

*I*n October 1946, with an office in Detroit, Michigan, and two employees, William Russell Kelly invented the modern temporary staffing industry to meet the office/clerical staffing needs of area businesses.

Today, Kelly Services® is a Fortune 500 giant and the leading provider of staffing services—providing more than 750,000 employees to 200,000 customers in 26 countries each year. On a daily basis, Kelly® puts approximately 150,000 temporary employees and 6,500 full-time employees to work through a network of more than 2,200 company-owned and -operated offices.

Mr. Kelly opened his first international office in Canada, the country of his birth, on June 1, 1968, at 250 Bloor Street East in central Toronto. Now, Kelly Services (Canada), Ltd., employs over 35,000 people per year through an extensive Canadian network of 52 offices from Nova Scotia to British Columbia—including its Mississauga flagship location at the centre

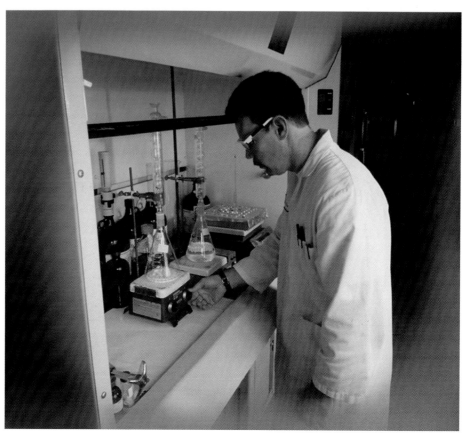

of the city. These offices share high standards of quality, consistency, delivery, service and onsite management expertise guaranteed by blanket ISO 9002 registration.

Kelly takes pride in providing highly qualified employees with a wide range of skill sets and has expanded its capabilities to include many other professional and technical disciplines, including accounting and finance, engineering, information technology, legal, scientific, marketing, manufacturing, distribution and call centre support.

Kelly Scientific Resources® staffs a full range of scientific specialists from entry-level to Ph.D. positions. Scientific employees can be placed in temporary, project and full-time positions in a variety of industries including pharmaceutical, biotechnology, chemical and food.

Kelly Scientific Resources' 80 plus branch offices are located worldwide and staffed and managed only by seasoned, degreed scientists and clinical professionals. More than 30 per cent have advanced or multiple degrees, with the average branch staff member having 12 years of applicable scientific experience. Kelly Scientific Resources has stayed ahead of the industry by offering a superior level of skilled employees and exceptional customer service—the first in the industry to offer the incentive of scientific employee training through the Internet!

Kelly Services' **Partnered Staffing** makes employing a large temporary workforce a cost-effective solution by appointing a single contact person onsite to focus on recruitment, retention and managing a contingent workforce. A Kelly onsite manager is a carefully selected staffing professional who is both motivated and prepared to advance company priorities.

Kelly **MultiHire**™ is the solution for companies that need to hire a large volume of permanent employees. Ideal for new facility openings and expansions, Kelly MultiHire helps facilitate job fairs, applicant screening and evaluation, interviews and reference checks, all designed to reflect each clients' particular organizational needs and ensure the best qualified candidates are identified for hire.

Kelly **Permanent Recruitment**, available at all Kelly branches throughout Canada, has successfully networked and matched thousands of candidates with full-time jobs. When clients approach Kelly with their open positions, candidates are identified with both the aptitude and the attitude necessary to succeed in each company's culture and environment. Kelly Permanent

Recruitment's direct placement puts the selected candidate on the customer's payroll immediately and is backed by a 90-day guarantee, so the decision to hire is virtually risk-free.

Kelly Services has received countless recognition by customers, community organizations and the business press for workplace diversity, quality processes, community involvement and management practices. In recent years these awards included: "Readers Choice Gold Award," *Toronto Sun*; "Consumer's Choice Gold Award," "Best Business Services Company for the 1990s," *Forbes* magazine; Ford Motor Company's Q1 Preferred Quality Award; DaimlerChrysler's Quality Excellence Award; Xerox Certified Supplier Award; and Kraft Food's first annual Rick Stuedemann Award for Supplier Excellence.

Moving ahead into the new millennium, Kelly Services will continue to provide the highest value possible to its employees, customers and stockholders through continuous innovation, expansion and exceptional customer service. ❖

City of Mississauga EDO

Mississauga is a distinct major Canadian city with a population of 605,600. As Canada's seventh largest city, it is considered a municipal leader in fiscal responsibility, technology and urban development. Mississauga provides its citizens with state-of-the-art facilities and programs and is recognized as the safest city in Canada to live, work and play.

Located in the heart of Mississauga, the distinctive Civic Centre houses local government services and hosts civic events.

We have all the right connections for long-term prosperity; Mississauga is home to an excellent multi-cultural workforce and continues to provide attractive business opportunities. The City has exceeded $1 billion in the value of building permits for the last number of years capitalizing on the strong Canadian economy.

Mississauga as a business location is very cost competitive. Property taxes are among the lowest in Ontario and the very active development industry has kept lease rates and land prices competitive. The city's utility rates are among the lowest in the GTA.

Many years of strong financial management by a series of Mississauga councils, plus a sustained drive for overall excellence in administration, are reflected in high quality municipal services. The City is debt-free with millions of dollars in reserve.

An ideal place for business definitely, but more importantly it is also a great diverse community. Mississauga is a great place to live with strong communities, a wide selection of excellent housing, shopping and great schools. There is an active cultural life with galleries, theatres, art centres, concert halls and museums including the Living Arts Centre. There are outstanding sports facilities, including the Hershey Centre, Lakeview and Britannia golf clubs and numerous community centres situated strategically throughout the city.

The beautiful Credit River valley provides scenic recreational parkland and its clean waters are excellent for fishing. Boating, from canoes to yachts, is a popular sport in Mississauga with three beautiful new marinas along the shores of Lake Ontario. There are over 400 parks, and you can hike, walk, in-line skate, ski and bike along more than 18 major trails along stream valleys, through woodlots or on the shores of Lake Ontario.

More than 40 Fortune 500 companies have their Canadian head offices in Mississauga. The city is well known for its strength in attracting major pharmaceutical firms such as GlaxoSmithKline and AstraZeneca. Mississauga also has a reputation as the home for advanced technology excellence including such firms as Hewlett-Packard, Microsoft, Bell and Oracle to name just a few. In addition, major automotive companies such as Nissan, Subaru and Daimler-Chrysler have a strong presence in Mississauga.

Logistics firms, shipping services such as FedEx and Purolator, aerospace and aviation industries including Boeing Toronto Ltd., Pratt & Whitney and Air Canada, as well the RBC Financial Services, CIBC Insurance, Dun and Bradstreet Canada and many other major financial institutions, all call Mississauga home.

Located in Mississauga, L. B. Pearson International Airport (LBPIA), a major hub and the busiest airport in the country, handles one-third of all scheduled flights within Canada, over half of Canada's international and U.S. traffic and more than 40 per cent of Canada's air cargo. Its location is especially convenient for those in Mississauga who travel frequently or who use air cargo shipments. By 2005, 33.2 million people are expected to travel through LBPIA. Currently 60 airlines provide non-stop service to 114 destinations in 44 countries from LBPIA.

As the only city within the Greater Toronto Area with seven major highways traversing it, Mississauga offers fast and convenient access to prime destinations in Canada and the United States. Businesses find they save considerable time and money with easy access to highways #401, 403, 407, 409, 410, 427 and the Queen Elizabeth Way (QEW). Mississauga also has excellent rail service.

The city offers services that will support the most demanding of corporate requirements. Business parks are cabled to accommodate state-of-the-art telecommunications facilities. Mississauga's telecommunications infrastructure is one of the most sophisticated in Canada. The city offers 100 per cent digital switching using state-of-the-art technology, simultaneous network facilities with fibre cable in all business parks and fully diverse, restorable fibre ring technologies.

An educated and enthusiastic workforce, a strategic location, low taxes and utility costs, room to grow, a quality educational system, a lively cultural scene, pleasant, safe residential neighbourhoods in a tolerant multicultural environment and excellent transportation and telecommunications links.

Mississauga has all the right connections! ❖

One of the largest commercial office complexes in Canada, the RBC Financial Group recently opened its major administrative centre in Mississauga.

Pallett Valo, LLP

*P*allett Valo LLP is a business law firm—we provide legal advice to businesses and to the people who own, run and manage them. Because we are a firm of business people with sound legal expertise, our approach is to offer understandable legal advice within a practical business context.

Our clients operate exciting enterprises. They range in size from small growth ventures—both new and old economy—to established public companies, professional partnerships, not-for-profit organizations, municipalities, trusts and estates and financial institutions.

We are told that we "get it" at all levels throughout our firm. This is of real benefit to our clients. We get that businesses are run by people, and that we must meet the individual's needs as well as their business needs. The lawyers and team members at Pallett Valo realize that in law, a keen understanding of the human side of business is vital to the continuing success of our clients.

We get that our clients want business-based solutions to issues and opportunities they encounter that have legal ramifications.

We get that we are in business to help our clients through the labyrinth of law to achieve their goals.

All of which means that we get service. We understand that as a law firm we are in the service industry, and that this service is defined by our clients.

Clients are served through six main divisions within the firm— corporate and commercial, litigation, labor and employment, real estate, construction and personal legal services.

Within this framework we have developed expertise in a number of specialized areas. We are able to work effectively with clients on routine every-day legal matters and, where required, provide guidance on complex corporate legal strategy or deal with complex litigation—both at the trial and appellate levels.

At a personal level, we help clients manage and protect their assets through insightful estate planning. As the population demographics continue to mature, we are increasingly involved in the complex issues relating to business succession planning.

Who are our clients? They are drawn from a cross section of many different industry sectors and business types. They are owners, executives, franchisors and in-house counsel.

They all have one thing in common—they want to succeed. ❖

Pallett Valo, LLP, a firm of business people with sound legal expertise.

The Office People Business Centres

Downsizing—or resizing as those who are making the staff cuts prefer to say—has left thousands of skilled and able bodied Canadians looking for work. Increasingly, those set adrift are seeking refuge from the rigors of job hunting by setting up their own small businesses.

Some experts predict that within 10 years more than half of the Canadian workforce will be 'small' businesses, operated primarily from home offices. But working out of the house doesn't suit everyone. While some people adapt easily, others find the easy going environment more of a distraction than an asset.

That's where companies like The Office People Business Centres fill a void.

The Office People features an entire floor of executive suites, which offer all the amenities of the traditional workplace combined with the flexibility most entrepreneurs value. At The Office People, centrally located in the economic hub of Mississauga at Highways #5 and #10, you can rent office space by the hour, the day, month or year—and it comes complete with furniture, secretarial support if and when necessary, a well equipped kitchen and free indoor parking.

Customers only pay for the services they use, as they use them. Every office is fully furnished, so all they need to get started is a computer. And if customers don't have one of those, The Office People will rent them one.

The Office People offer an excellent Business Identity Package consisting of a phone number, personal call answering, custom greeting in your company's

An impressive lobby with contemporary décor.

name, call forwarding, call patching, voice mail, prestigious business address, mail and package handling and a personal keyed mailbox. This service allows companies to have a presence in Mississauga without actually renting an office or requiring local staff. Billing is done in 15-minute increments, a real cost saving to small businesses on a tight budget.

Occupying an executive suite helps a small business owner portray a professional image because The Office People's offices are all tastefully decorated and the large 12-seat boardroom has all the amenities one would expect of a large corporation—a 32-inch television, VCR and white board.

The Office People even has a full line of business staples in stock. There are huge private lockers for storing bulky items and a copy centre with high-speed photocopying and faxing services available. They even offer a full line of marketing services for those who don't have the time or skills to do it themselves. Services include printing, telemarketing, flyer distribution and promotional items.

One of the side benefits of occupying an Office People executive suite is the opportunity to network with others just like you. The contacts clients have made while getting a cup of coffee have frequently led to business associations between small business operators.

The Office People's executive suites offer all the advantages of a big business at small business rates. ❖

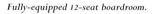

Fully-equipped 12-seat boardroom.

Lyons Auto Body Ltd.

When Jack Lyons moved his fledgling auto repair business to its present location almost 50 years ago, the 860 feet of frontage north of the village of Erindale was one and a half miles from the nearest main highway. In front of the building was a little-travelled concession road, while all around were hay fields occupied by grazing cattle.

Now, Lyons Auto Body Ltd. is in the middle of Mississauga, Canada's seventh largest city. More than 600,000 people reside within a leisurely 20-minute drive of Lyons' Burnhamthorpe location, just east of Creditview. The business has grown from its humble beginnings behind the house where Jack lived to become North America's largest auto body operation.

A recent 8,000-square-foot expansion has increased the total size of the operation to more than 35,000 square feet, where about 100 employees and a fleet of tow trucks service the Mississauga area. His son John Lyons and daughter Valerie Lyons-Sala are both involved in the business.

The company's fleet of 25 yellow-colored wheel lift tow trucks—both light and heavy duty—is a familiar site in Mississauga. Each is radio dispatched and is available for either short or long hauls. Lyons also has flatbed trucks for severely damaged vehicles or transporting classic vehicles. Lyons is capable of tackling any towing or recovery job any time, anywhere, 24 hours a day, 365 days a year.

Lyons offers "one-stop," 24-hour collision assistance and state-of-the-art claims handling services, including computerized estimating and photo

Jack Lyons and staff in 2001.

imaging technology, accompanied by online data transfer with insurance providers, a customer shuttle service and commercial truck repair and towing. Lyons has its own fleet of late model rental vehicles on site.

Lyons' certified *I-Car* Gold Class technicians employ the GENESIS two-laser measuring technology to guarantee that all vehicles are repaired to manufacturer's specifications. Lyons uses Sikkens Paint, applied in three downdraft spray booths to ensure a factory-baked paint finish. Certified mechanical technicians use state-of-the-art John Bean 3D Visualiner diagnosis and alignment technology to repair all suspension damage. All collision repairs receive a lifetime warranty for as long as the customer owns the vehicle.

Many Lyons employees have been with the firm more than 30 years and a few have retired, never having had a job other than that at Lyons Auto Body Ltd. Employees are key to Lyons' success, Jack says. "You concentrate on giving the customer quality work, treat your employees well, make sure they are well trained and keep up with the times.

"A satisfied customer will come back the next time and will tell his friends and family. It's really a partnership between Lyons, the insurance companies, our employees and the customer. We're all working together to provide quality service." ❖

Jack Lyons and staff in 1958.

Merrill Lynch

Merrill Lynch is one of the world's leading financial management and advisory companies with more than a century of history, culture and heritage. Merrill Lynch Canada Inc., member CIPF, on Robert Speck Parkway in the heart of Mississauga, advises individuals, corporations, institutions and governments on how best to achieve their financial goals.

In Mississauga, Merrill Lynch enjoys a remarkable reputation built over the years by the company's commitment to service excellence, client focus and local expertise. The company's tradition dates back to 1885, providing the strong foundation to help the staff meet the challenges of today's rapidly changing business environment.

Since 1952, Merrill Lynch has been providing investment-banking services to Canadians. In 1998, the firm became a full-service brokerage firm by extending its services to individual investors. With more than 4,000 employees across Canada, Merrill Lynch is uniquely positioned to offer clients world-class guidance and support.

In Canada, 1,300 financial consultants in 130 branch offices work closely with more than 600,000 investors. A team of more than 30 investment research professionals focuses on 300 of the top Canadian companies. Merrill Lynch Canada has built a reputation for excellence by always putting clients' interests first.

The Mississauga office, which opened March 8, 1993, has a staff of 40 including Brad Shoemaker, Kathy Shoemaker, Phil Sanders, John Enright, Taras Hucal, Andy Kim, Dean Colling, Drew Pallett and John Speck.

The management group believes in giving back to the community. Brad and Kathy Shoemaker are involved in Child Find; Brad Shoemaker is a Scout leader and a member of the steering committee of the Community Foundation of Mississauga. Phil Sanders coaches hockey, is involved in local school programs and assists the local swim club. John Enright is involved with Big Brothers of Peel, is a member of the Canadian Ski Patrol and works with the United Way. Andy Kim coaches lacrosse; Dean Colling coaches minor hockey and is a contributing financial columnist with The Mississauga Business Times.

Drew Pallett is vice-chair of the Mississauga Living Arts Centre and John Speck is involved with the Trillium Health Centre, the Mississauga Heritage Foundation, the Mississauga Symphony, the Schizophrenia Society and Community Foundation of Mississauga.

"Our clients' needs are growing progressively more complex," Brad Shoemaker says. "To help serve our clients, we continue to invest in our resources and in professional development programs, careful supervision and mentoring. Merrill Lynch's best investment has always been in its people.

"We have an outstanding group of people in the Mississauga branch. We recognize that each client is unique. We work as a team, sharing ideas and information across geographic borders and organizational boundaries to help clients achieve their goals. But we realize that to do our best for clients, we have to know and understand the community in which they live and work. That's why we feel it's important to become involved in community activities."❖

Merrill Lynch's Private Client Group outside the Mississauga office at 186 Robert Speck Parkway—committed to the community of Mississauga

Turner & Porter Funeral Directors Limited

Turner & Porter Funeral Directors Limited has been serving west Toronto and Mississauga for more than 127 years and is Ontario's largest independent funeral home. The firm is still operated by a Porter. Douglas Porter, president, is a fourth generation descendant of Thomas Porter, who joined his father-in-law Frederick Turner in 1881. They worked together until Turner's death in 1900.

When Thomas Porter died in 1927, his son Fred Porter took over. F. Ray Porter joined the business in 1934, and his sons Rick and Doug later followed in their father's footsteps. Doug Porter became sole owner when Rick died in 1984.

Today, Turner & Porter serves more than 2,400 families annually from four west-end locations. Following two westerly moves along Queen Street, the location on Roncesvalles Avenue in Parkdale, was acquired in 1919. In 1957, the Yorke Chapel at 2357 Bloor Street West, near Jane Street, was purchased. In 1967, the Peel Chapel at 2180 Hurontario Street in Mississauga, just north of the Queen Elizabeth Way, was built, and the Butler Chapel on Dundas Street at Islington Avenue in Etobicoke was purchased in 1988.

While each location differs in detail, all Turner & Porter funeral homes share common characteristics—a spacious foyer, quietly but comfortably furnished reception suites, private family room and a chapel with adjoining family room.

A typical example of the firm's thoughtful care and attention is one that transcends purely business considerations—the Turner & Porter Community Awareness Centre. The centre offers a bereavement support group called Community of People Extending Support (COPES), which provides a

(Above) The Turner & Porter "Peel Chapel" situated at 2180 Hurontario Street, just north of the Q.E.W.

vehicle for recovery after loss. The centre sponsors seminars for health-care professionals, schools, senior citizens organizations and community groups, dealing with various aspects of funerals and bereavement. It also maintains a lending library of books, brochures and video tapes.

Turner & Porter was invited to join Selected Independent Funeral Homes in 1949, an international organization dedicated to meeting the highest standards in funeral service. F. Ray Porter was its first Canadian President from 1959 to 1960. The organization has also been a leader in the area of funeral preplanning. Turner & Porter's Preplanning Centre was opened in 1985.

Recently, Turner & Porter introduced a virtual memory board, a history of the deceased person that can be placed on the Internet.

"We never forget," Porter says, "that we are literally providing a temporary 'home' for the families we serve, and we spare no effort to provide a home environment. Our goal is to work as a team to help families begin the healing process after the loss of a loved one. Our future, like our past, will be based on the simple philosophy of dignified service and giving people what they need." ❖

(Below) The spacious entrance foyer of the "Peel Chapel."

Chapter Ten

❖

COMMUNICATIONS & BROADCASTING

Photo by Michael Scholz

Rogers Cable Inc.

*T*here are few Mississauga residents who have not been touched in some way by Rogers' group of companies.

Rogers Communications Inc. is a communications, entertainment and information company consisting of numerous businesses, each a leader in its respective field. Rogers Cable Inc. provides cable television, high-speed Internet access and digital cable. Rogers Video is the largest Canadian video retail business. Rogers AT&T Wireless is involved in cellular, Digital PCS, paging and data communications and Rogers Media Inc. is involved in new media businesses, radio and television broadcasting, tele-shopping and publishing.

Rogers is now involved in professional sports as well, having purchased Major League Baseball's Toronto Blue Jays and the Toronto Phantom indoor football club.

Rogers Cable came to Mississauga in 1972 when it acquired the various local cable organizations. Six years later, Rogers Cable had more than 203,000 customers in Toronto, East York, Scarborough, Etobicoke, Mississauga, Brampton, Caledon and Essex County. At present the company has 2.3 million customers in Ontario, New Brunswick and Newfoundland.

Rogers has one of the most advanced Hybrid Fibre Coaxial (HFC) networks in North America, optimizing the features of both fibre-optic and coaxial cable. This advanced network allows Rogers to deliver high-quality entertainment, information and communication services.

Rogers provides in-home entertainment including digital television programming pictured below.

Rogers was the first cable operator in North America to introduce Interactive Television (ITV), thus allowing customers to surf the Internet through their television sets. New technologies continue to be researched and include Video On Demand (VOD) and Internet Protocol (IP) Telephony.

VOD will allow customers to choose when they want to watch television programming (not subjected to channel scheduling). Accessed through an Interactive Program Guide, customers will be able to view, pause and rewind (just like a VCR). IP Telephony is to be introduced to the multi-dwelling unit (apartments and condominiums) marketplace over the next few years. IP Telephony provides telephone services over the Internet via the cable network.

While its mission is to provide customers with the most advanced entertainment and communication technologies available, Rogers equally believes in the importance of supporting and serving the communities it serves—with special emphasis on youth and education.

Launched in 1995, Cable In The Classroom (CITC) was conceived and designed to provide Canadian teachers with an additional teaching tool to enhance their curriculum. Since that time, Rogers has spent more than $3 million placing cable in more than 2,500 schools—that's over 88 per cent of all publicly funded elementary and secondary schools in the Rogers' service areas. Through CITC, Rogers brings 37 networks and over 360 hours of copyright-cleared, commercial-free, educational cable television programming to teachers for use in the classroom every month.

Rogers also provides support to the local community through corporate funding and the individual participation of employees. Probably its best-known community-based initiative is the Rogers Pumpkin Patrol, which has been operating for more than 15 years to help keep kids safe on Halloween.

The company's bright red vans patrol local streets with employee volunteers who are equipped with cellular phones. They work with the local police to spot trick-or-treaters needing assistance. During the two weeks prior to Halloween, employees distribute safety loot packs, which include a safety-tips card and reflective armband to many schools. In addition, some schools receive a Rogers safety presentation in partnership with local police.

Through Rogers@Home, which provides high-speed Internet access through cable, Rogers is committed to Internet safety and is a strong supporter of the Media Awareness Network (MNet), a non-profit organization dedicated to supporting media literacy and Internet education. The MNet Web site offers user-friendly resources and information on a variety of media-related topics such as advertising and commercialism, media violence and the media's portrayal of gender. The objective is to teach children to be Internet Smart.

In addition, in the Peel Region, Rogers has spent $1.5 million to provide 300 schools with computers, printers and three years of complimentary

As seen below Rogers continuously upgrades and maintains its network to the highest standards.

The power of coaxial cable allows customers to receive television programming, internet access and in the future telephone service.

high-speed access to the Internet via the Rogers@Home service as part of the Rogers@School Program.

Rogers Television (channel 10 in Mississauga) brings communities together. For more than 30 years, Rogers Cable has invested in the creation and development of Rogers Television. Each Rogers Television station is an active and involved member of the communities it serves. Rogers trains thousands of volunteers, who work side by side with professional television producers to bring unique local programming. Rogers Television is only available on cable, which provides Rogers with a unique competitive advantage.

The quality of Rogers' programming is exemplary. It was recently recognized with four prestigious international prizes at the *2000 Hometown Video Festival Awards*. Its production, reflecting back on the 1979 Mississauga trail derailment, received top marks in the document event category.

Rogers has always been proud to be a part of the Mississauga community, taking great pride in the products and services it offers to the residents of Mississauga. Unquestionably, Rogers believes in putting its customers first. ❖

The Shopping Channel

For more than 10 years, Canadians from coast to coast have embraced The Shopping Channel (tSc), Canada's only nationally televised, 24-hour shop-at-home service. The channel reaches into six million households across the country and has a loyal audience of two million viewers weekly.

Developed in 1987, the Mississauga-based company truly took flight in 1996 as its ownership and broadcast style changed. The Shopping Channel severed its ties with former partners and became wholly owned and operated by Rogers Communications, thus developing its own software and trademarks.

Today, The Shopping Channel is a Canadian success story that continues to evolve. With sales of $200 million in 2000, the channel currently receives more than 80,000 calls per week, sends out approximately 40,000 packages a week and employs 600 people.

Canadian merchandise and on-air personalities add to the flavor of The Shopping Channel experience. Although the channel is not limited to selling Canadian goods, it features many homegrown products from companies based in regions across the country.

In 1999, The Shopping Channel launched www.TheShoppingChannel.com, an e-commerce retail Web site that became profitable within the first nine months of operation. Also in 1999, tSc launched an expanded new catalogue and its first brick-and-motor retail store.

Subsequently, in 2000 tSc launched the Alex and Zoe Toy Store at TheShoppingChannel.com, Canada's most comprehensive home shopping toy resource. In a 2001 e-tailing survey conducted by Deloitte and Touche which rated customer satisfaction, timely deliveries and repeat visits,

The Shopping Channel offers customers the choice of shopping on-air, online at TheShoppingChannel.com or from its recently expanded catalogue.

TheShoppingChannel.com was ranked Canada's number one homegrown "e-tail blazer".

All of these initiatives have proved successful, and along with the development of a new Mississauga broadcast facility, The Shopping Channel will continue to move its business forward in the years to come. ❖

The Shopping Channel broadcasts live from its studio in Mississauga.

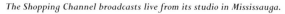

Transcontinental Printing

As readers leaf through the pages of this book, one thing will be obvious to even the most casual observer—the quality of reproduction and printing is outstanding.

Transcontinental Printing wouldn't have it any other way—especially since it is not only responsible for production of this book, but its own corporate profile is included. As one of the top 10 printers in the world, and the second largest in Canada, Transcontinental is justifiably proud of its work.

A corporate culture with a long-standing commitment to quality and customer service has been responsible for the wide and diverse line-up of important companies with whom Transcontinental works. The duration and diversity of many of these relationships is a testimony to the success of the company's business philosophy.

From leading retailers such as The Bay, Zellers, Home Hardware and Oshawa Foods, to consumer publications such as Saturday Night and The Hockey News, the names of the customers who rely on Transcontinental Printing are plentiful enough to fill a telephone directory—and Transcontinental produces several of those, as well. In fact, the average Canadian likely touches some piece of paper printed by Transcontinental every day.

Transcontinental's traditional focus on high-end, high volume and high-quality printing—flyers, catalogues, magazines, directories, books, brochures, annual reports and newspapers—has evolved through acquisition and emerging technologies to encompass other complementary communications sectors: distribution, publishing and technologies such as the manufacture of audio CDs and CD-ROMs.

High-tech computer systems operate each of Transcontinental's massive multi-million dollar press lines, ensuring optimum quality and total customer satisfaction.

Transcontinental Printing employs over 600 highly skilled people at its three Mississauga area plant locations. The Brampton facility, shown here, specializes in newspaper insert products that are distributed daily across Canada and the northeast United States.

In publishing, Transcontinental Publications is a leader in specialized and new trend publications. This division has evolved from a magazine and newspaper publisher into an overall information provider, expanding into areas such as direct marketing and electronic publishing.

Transcontinental has always been at the forefront in incorporating the latest equipment to make the printing, binding and distribution processes more efficient. The Printing Division also encompasses electronic prepress for direct computer-to-plate production, eliminating the need of traditional film required for plate making. Complete finishing, shipping services and direct mail capabilities are available across North America from more than 40 manufacturing facilities.

Each plant and division has its own areas of expertise. By producing work in the plant that is best suited to the customer's requirements, whether in the Mississauga area or elsewhere, Transcontinental can better control costs and turnaround. This approach also offers customers a full range of printing and communications-related services at the local, regional or international level.

Transcontinental Printing is proud of its more than 11,500 employees, its capabilities and its success in working with clients to help them to fulfill their diverse and evolving communications needs. ❖

Chapter Eleven

11

HEALTH CARE, EDUCATION & QUALITY OF LIFE

Photo by Michael Scholz

University of Toronto at Mississauga

$\mathcal{E}$nrolment growth and expansion best describe the University of Toronto at Mississauga (UTM) as it heads into the new millennium. An integral part of the western GTA since 1967, UTM has produced 26,000 graduates and contributes significantly to Mississauga's well-educated work force.

UTM, with a current enrolment of 6,500 full- and part-time students, pairs the strength and international reputation of the University of Toronto with a modern, mid-size campus situated in a comfortable urban setting. U of T Mississauga students are part of the community of Nobel Prize winners, Canadian prime ministers, world-class novelists, renowned researchers and astronauts, and they have access to the resources of one of the world's elite universities. In North America, U of T's library system is ranked among the top five universities for its holdings of books, periodicals, digital resources and other reference materials.

Academic programs led by dedicated scholars and researchers are the mark of a great university. UTM offers 125 programs in 70 areas of study.

UTM's new first-year residence complex won the City of Mississauga 2000 Urban Design Award of Excellence. Cited for its overall design and quality of construction, the building represents an innovative approach in helping new students adapt to residence life. Another new campus building, The Student Centre, was named one of nine Millennium Design Icon buildings in Mississauga—recognized for its architecture, both inside and out, and its community and open space design.

Excellent student services have long been a trademark of the UTM campus. The university provides 24-hour access to computer labs and has internet service in all its residences, a career centre, disability services, internship and mentorship programs, and the Academic Skills Centre, a unique "support centre" designed to help students develop academic skills for a higher degree of success in their studies.

Unique interdisciplinary combinations are encouraged—including communication, culture and information technology, and forensics, environmental studies, biotechnology, world perspectives and second language teaching. Its two masters programs, the master of management and professional accounting and master of biotech, combine a strong academic base with work term placements in some of the country's leading financial institutions and pharmaceutical companies.

UTM is continually being recognized for its strengths and applauded for its unique approach to both undergraduate and graduate programming. Its two newest buildings (the Student Centre and first-year residence complex) won urban design awards of excellence, its faculty has earned provincial and national recognition, and it has received millions of dollars in federal and provincial research grants and financial support from business, industry and the City of Mississauga.

Within the next 5 to 10 years, UTM expects to undergo extraordinary changes. It's anticipated that enrolment will jump by 50 per cent or more. In order to meet that challenge, UTM has developed a new master plan to address the issues of growth. The plan will connect the culture of the campus with the natural environment in a way that fosters interaction and offers a vision for the expanded campus.

Leading the way is UTM's new communication, culture and information technology (CCIT) facility, a $32 million, state-of-the-art building and a program offered jointly with Sheridan College of Oakville. The building will provide a fully wired digital media teaching environment, equipped for the most advanced Internet and intranet communication. The facility will also contain a large lecture theatre, faculty offices and research laboratories.

CCIT is an extension of a long-standing successful partnership between UTM and Sheridan College. This new program will be the third partnership between these two institutions—an art and art history and theatre and drama program are the other joint offerings. CCIT will again capitalize on the strengths of both institutions to create a totally unique program that will offer academic, research and employment opportunities to students, faculty and partners while creating a new generation of communications professionals who are effective, polished and prepared to work in positions where communications, knowledge and skills are prized—as corporate spokespersons, crisis managers, project leaders, technology facilitators, technical writers, team builders, cultural advisers and marketing strategists.

CCIT will be a four-year program leading to a joint University of Toronto/Sheridan undergraduate degree, either a bachelor of arts in communication or a bachelor of science in communication.

UTM's goal is to thrive within a world-class intellectual environment, to continue to attract both top scholars and students and to continue to link with partners in business and industry for the purpose of research and development in the pharmaceutical industry, medicine, finance, the environment and numerous other disciplines.

The university's programs will remain relevant, intellectually challenging and responsive to the ever-evolving demands of a global society. The University of Toronto at Mississauga is continuing to invest in both new programs and attracting outstanding faculty who will, in turn, draw the best students. It will continue to be the preeminent campus in Peel Region and one of the best universities anywhere. ❖

To meet the demands of the new media/high-tech information age, UTM developed the communication, culture and information technology (CCIT) program. This new four-year program has been designed to produce top-notch professionals energized to take up the challenges of the wired world. CCIT students will study the art and science of human communication, how communication builds knowledge and creates culture, and how information technology affects the way humans communicate. This program is offered jointly between the University of Toronto at Mississauga and Sheridan College in Oakville. It combines the academic research strength and international prestige of the U of T (at UTM) with the professional orientation and worldwide media reputation of Sheridan. CCIT will produce its first graduates in 2005.

CCIT is only one of many unique programs offered at UTM. Others include: the Rotman School of Management MMPA (master of management and professional accounting) program, forensic science, environmental studies, second language learning, the master of biotechnology and other joint programs with neighbouring Sheridan College in theatre and drama and art and art history.

UTM provides its students with the resources of the world's elite universities including the U of T library system, ranked in the top five universities in North America. UTM adds outstanding research facilities, smart classrooms and the Hitachi Research Lab—a state-of-the-art facility equipped with the latest computer hardware and computer-assisted telephone interviewing (CATI) software presently available for use in the design, implementation and analysis of social, consumer and marketing surveys.

UTM prides itself on faculty achievements in both teaching and research, and their accessibility to students. Its faculty members are educators and research scholars who not only contribute to new knowledge, but also explore their findings with students both in and outside of classes. In fact, UTM faculty have collectively won more Ontario Colleges and Universities Faculty Association (OCUFA) awards for teaching excellence than any other college or division at the U of T.

Sheridan College

ince Sheridan College opened in September 1967, it has grown from a small, locally based college of 400 students to the fifth largest college in Ontario with just over 11,000 full-time post-secondary and post-graduate students in 100 programs and 43,000 part-time students in 850 programs/courses.

Sheridan serves the communities of Oakville, Mississauga, Brampton and Burlington through its Trafalgar and Davis campuses and Skills Training Centre, but about 25 per cent of its students come from outside the Halton and Peel Regions. The student population includes representatives from 33 countries. There are 930 employees and more than 60,000 alumni.

Sheridan College is committed to meeting the growing and diverse educational needs of students through the provision of flexible and innovative learning opportunities, enabling students and employees to build productive careers and to excel in a changing society.

The Trafalgar Road campus is home to 6,500 students and offers programs in animation, arts and design; business; community and liberal studies; and computing and information management. The Trafalgar Road Campus includes an athletic facility, a Student Centre, library, cafeteria and other food outlets.

In Brampton, field placements and cooperative employment/education opportunities are available at the Davis campus, home to 4,500 students.

This is the SCAET Building, Sheridan Centre for Animation and Emerging Technologies at the Trafalgar Road Campus in Oakville. The building opened fall 2000.

Named after former Ontario Premier William Davis, Davis Campus is located in neighbouring Brampton.

Sheridan's business programs collaborate with the Brampton Chamber of Commerce while the science and technology programs are uniquely positioned to contribute to the industries growing rapidly within the Brampton area.

The Davis Campus features a 17,000-square-foot student centre, plus an athletic facility, library, full-service cafeteria and other food outlets.

All students choosing Sheridan have one reason in common: the desire to experience quality, world-class education. Sheridan's post-secondary and postgraduate programs prepare students for their chosen career through excellent classroom training and superior hands-on skills development. Business and industry representatives regularly advise Sheridan's professional teaching staff to ensure that programs and equipment feature the latest workplace technologies, developments and trends. Many faculty have worked in the professions they teach, thus providing students with valuable, first-hand perspectives on future careers.

Sheridan's emphasis on practical, quality training, relevant to the demands of the new millennium also impresses employers. Most recently, 93 per cent of graduates obtained employment upon graduation, while 92 per cent of employers expressed satisfaction with the Sheridan graduates they had hired.

In the past decade, public funding has dropped to 40 per cent, forcing Sheridan to look to other sources of funding—including the private sector—to sustain the quality of its educational programming. Sheridan realizes it must operate as a successful business, providing high-quality educational products and services to its clients, where, when and how they demand them.

Students enjoy mobile computing at the Trafalgar Road Campus Grounds.

Sheridan is at the forefront of enhanced learning opportunities for the new millennium. Programs incorporating mobile computing offer an innovative and student-centred learning experience. Students selecting mobile computing programs enjoy the use of a laptop computer for the duration of the academic term, as well as access to a wide variety of computer-based research and course materials. Students can exploit the full range of learning opportunities unique to mobile computing, including collaborative on-line work groups, Web-based research, subject-area chat rooms and electronic submissions. In most courses, students have access to course schedules, on-line tests, assignments, quizzes, topical outlines and a variety of different learning materials.

Sheridan's Trafalgar Road and Davis campuses are equipped with classrooms especially designed for mobile computer users, featuring specially designed tables, ergonomic chairs, large whiteboards, a network printer and overhead projection systems. The design of the classrooms stimulates group, team and collaborative work. "Network drops" and power outlets have been installed in hallways, libraries, study carrels and student centers—places that are conducive to individual or group work.

Sheridan, long known for its excellence in animation technology, recently opened a new $32 million, 85,000-square- foot facility at the Trafalgar Road Campus called the Sheridan Centre for Animation & Emerging Technologies (SCAET), funded through a combination of public and private sector investment.

SCAET is a state-of-the-art facility for everything from computer animation, interactive media, and digital special effects to online journalism and the development of new telecommunications technology, SCAET provides learning facilities for 1,200 full-time students who will study both at the Sheridan and University of Toronto Mississauga campuses. SCAET also houses the Visualization Design Institute, an applied research centre.

Partners not only contribute technology support, they bring a wealth of new ideas and talent to the centre. Sheridan bestows the title of "Adjunct Professor" on alumni who have demonstrated a commitment to working with Sheridan to enhance program quality. Among those who participate are former Academy Award nominees James Straus (*Dragonheart*) and Steve Williams (*The Mask*), who was responsible for animating the dinosaurs in the movie Jurassic Park.

The Sheridan Elder Research Centre (SERC) is an interdisciplinary, applied research initiative focused on issues associated with aging. SERC's approach is psychosocial in nature and geared to building on and reinforcing the strengths of Canada's aging population. SERC draws on the resources of related courses such as cosmetics techniques and management, interior design, crafts and design, and information technology.

Sheridan has a unique partnership with the region of Peel. Sheridan trained the supervisors of the region's 11 directly operated child-care centres in a program called High/Scope, which originated at the High/Scope Educational Research Foundation, an independent nonprofit research, development, training and public advocacy organization in Michigan. And, for the past several years, Sheridan has held up to nine convocation ceremonies each June at the Living Arts Centre in Mississauga.

In this world of rapid change and ambiguity, the advantage will go to those who risk setting their own vision and direction. Sheridan College is taking steps to ensure it continues to be the destination of choice for those seeking academic excellence, quality employment and opportunity for creative growth in the new millennium. ❖

Sheridan business students hard at work.

AstraZeneca Canada Inc.

A world leader in the pharmaceutical industry, AstraZeneca is a research-oriented company committed to innovation and dedicated to improving the health and quality of life for all Canadians. The extensive product portfolio spans seven therapeutic areas including gastrointestinal, oncology, respiratory, cardiovascular, central nervous system, infection and pain control.

The company's extensive range of products makes significant contributions to treatment options and patient care. AstraZeneca's brands include Nexium®, Losec®, Atacand®, Merrem®, Arimidex®, Zoladex®, Seroquel®, Zomig®, Diprivan® and Pulmicort®.

AstraZeneca is a major global employer. Worldwide, the company employs more than 50,000 in 150 countries. Over 25,000 people work in global sales and marketing. Meanwhile, 12,000 people are employed in production in 20 countries.

AstraZeneca Canada Inc. employs more than 1,400 people across Canada. The company's head office complex, located in Mississauga, Ontario, houses more than 815 employees working in manufacturing, administration, clinical research, sales, marketing and distribution.

In addition, more than 100 dedicated and highly skilled scientists work at AstraZeneca's state-of-the-art basic research centre in Montreal. Opened in 1997, AstraZeneca R&D Montreal is one of nine major drug discovery centers that AstraZeneca maintains worldwide. Scientists at the facility are focused on finding new and innovative therapeutic solutions to treat acute and chronic pain. The Montreal facility is a cornerstone of the company's vision to become a global leader in the overall therapeutic area of pain control.

A fully integrated company, AstraZeneca head office employees work in manufacturing, administration, clinical research, sales, marketing and distribution.

AstraZeneca Canada Inc. employs over 1,400 people across Canada.

Much of AstraZeneca's success in becoming a leader in the pharmaceutical industry has been achieved by its outstanding commitment to research and development. Through this research, AstraZeneca constantly strives to find new and better therapies.

Worldwide, the company employs more than 10,000 R&D personnel and invests $10 million US every working day on research and development, totaling $2.4 billion US per year. In Canada, AstraZeneca invests more than $1.5 million CDN each week in the pursuit of new therapies.

As a research oriented company, AstraZeneca believes curiosity is the best way to express its commitment to patient health. Looking beyond the obvious and solving problems in innovative ways—this is what drives the researchers the company supports and AstraZeneca scientists forward in their hunt for new and better treatments for a wide array of medical conditions and diseases.

AstraZeneca prides itself on being a leader in promoting research throughout Canada. The AstraZeneca Research Award program is a multi-million dollar initiative that works in co-operation with the Canadian Institutes of Health Research, Canada's Research-Based Pharma-ceutical Companies Research Program and a number of national health organizations. The Research Award program is designed to fund basic research projects by up-and-coming scientists at Canadian universities and medical institutions.

More than 100 dedicated and highly skilled scientists work at the basic research facility in Montreal.

AstraZeneca Canada Inc. also sponsors chairs in Organic Synthesis, Biotechnology, Respirology, Cardiovascular Research, Respiratory Disease Management and Breast Cancer at leading universities across Canada.

Such partnerships provide outstanding training opportunities for talented young researchers as well as world-renowned scientists. They also allow AstraZeneca to strengthen its ties with industry and the academic community and to have access to cutting-edge research.

AstraZeneca also pursues strategic research collaborations with external companies and academic institutions to support and enhance its drug discovery and development programs.

The company is also involved in developing and sponsoring accredited and non-accredited post-graduate courses for family physicians in Ontario and across Canada to teach patient management of diseases in the respiratory, gastrointestinal, central nervous system and cardiovascular areas.

AstraZeneca is a staunch believer in corporate social responsibility and is committed to the communities in which its employees live and conduct business. The company is committed to the well being of the whole patient, not just the disease. At the local, national and international level, AstraZeneca supports a wide range of charitable, educational and environmental initiatives.

As an Imagine Caring Company, AstraZeneca Canada Inc. commits to donating a minimum of one per cent of pretax profits to community organizations, and to encouraging employee volunteering in the community.

The company supports several national and local charitable initiatives. Each year, its employees participate in the Canadian Breast Cancer Foundation's Run for the Cure to raise funds for breast cancer research. The company also supports the United Way of Peel Region, Centraide of Greater Montreal and the Starlight Children's Foundation.

AstraZeneca also actively supports a wide range of local educational programs and health organizations. In Ontario, AstraZeneca Canada Inc. works closely with the ACT Foundation to encourage the Ontario government to make CPR training a mandatory part of the student curriculum.

The company supports various community initiatives including the City of Mississauga's Canada Day celebration for families, the Mississauga Arts Council, the Living Arts Centre and the Mississauga Library.

Internally, AstraZeneca Canada Inc.'s national charitable giving program, *Side by Side*, encourages, acknowledges and financially supports employees' personal involvement and voluntary contributions to different charitable organizations. It's part of the company's commitment to improving health and quality of life in Canada.

For more information about AstraZeneca Canada Inc. visit its Web site at www.astrazeneca.ca. ❖

AstraZeneca is a staunch believer in corporate social responsibility and is committed to the communities in which its employees live and conduct business.

Centre for Education and Training

The Centre for Education and Training (CET) is Peel Region's—if not all of Canada's—best kept secret when it comes to training and education.

This "not-for-profit" corporation, in association with the Peel District School Board, is a dynamic organization dedicated to enhancing both individual self-sufficiency and organizational effectiveness through its different career resource services. It is a complete service organization that provides limitless resources in the field of education and training for the community and beyond.

CET started in 1989 with six staff working out of 1,200 square feet of space at the Peel Region Board of Education offices. Now, it has more than 300 full time staff who generate more than $27 million in revenue annually. There are five distinct divisions and 20 locations throughout Ontario.

CET is providing service to over 600,000 people every year and has expanded to such places as Mexico, South America, Cuba, China, Japan, Korea and Europe. Recently, CET signed agreements with the governments of China and South Korea to provide language training, computer training and corporate training as well as online learning.

"We're bridging the gap between education and employment," Jim Gollert, chief executive officer says proudly. "We're very much about people; we're very customer focused, whether it is an individual looking for help in preparing a resume or a large corporation turning to us for help in resizing, developing team building or preparing workplace harassment guidelines."

The Centre for Language Training and Assessment (CLTA)

CLTA provides individual and corporate clients with a complete range of language programs and services including translation and interpretation, English language assessment and training, and academic upgrading. Staff work closely with clients to identify training needs, establish learning goals and equip them with the communication and critical-thinking tools needed for success in today's workplace.

Programs are delivered at sites conveniently located throughout the region of Peel, at a client's workplace or online. Flexible delivery schedules allow clients to find the programs best suited to their needs.

The Career Path Institute (CPI)

The Career Path Institute develops and delivers a number of services and programs focused on enhancing individual's career planning and job search skills. Services include resource and career centres, jobs search and mentoring programs for adults and youth, employment-focused trade shows and numerous other programs and services to assist those making choices about their careers or conducting a job search.

The Computer Technology Institute (CTI)

Clients often comment that the instructors at the Computer Technology Institute are the best anywhere. The instructors' experience in industry and in teaching adults helps make training practical and relevant to today's workplace.

CTI develops and delivers computer-training solutions geared to the needs of individuals and business. Programs range from customized flexible corporate training to part-time I.T. training programs to full-time career training programs. I.T. programs are offered in specific areas—software applications, technical specialization, programming, Web design, e-commerce, accounting, publishing and presentation. CTI's excellence in instruction and modern training facilities build skills to meet the demands of tomorrow's I.T. training challenges.

There are training facilities located in Mississauga, Brampton and Toronto. Training labs and software are upgraded regularly to ensure that students are using the latest available technology. A computer is available for each client at an ergonomically designed workstation. A maximum of 20 students attend classes in these facilities but options for on-site training at the client's location make for a variety of flexible training options.

Innovations Media (IM)

Innovations Media develops computer-based learning solutions through engaging, interactive, instructional design and can translate any content into an effective learning system. IM overcomes difficult and complex learning challenges through its understanding of the learning process, a mastery of e-learning technologies and a dedication to meeting the needs of the learner and/or the client.

Quality and Continuous Improvement Centre (QCIC)

QCIC provides a full range of services to meet and exceed any organization's needs. Staff members have expertise in assessing both corporate and employee needs, can identify blockages and training requirements at all levels company-wide and can clearly determine the strengths and aptitudes of all individuals who, in today's global market, must be an integral part of the change process. They have the tools and expertise to assess aptitude and interests as well as personal, academic and technological skill levels.

All training is personalized to meet the specific needs of the clientele. QCIC's programs have serviced more than 10,000 individuals in the past three years.

Employment Services operates under an HRDC program designed to match qualified job seekers to permanent, full-time continuous employment for residents of Peel, Halton and Dufferin regions.

"If someone needs assistance, the Centre for Education and Training can help," Gollert says. "If we continue to grow at the current rate and focus on our core businesses, I expect our revenues to increase two to three fold over the next few years."❖

Carter-Horner Inc.

Carter-Horner Inc. has more than 75 years of history in manufacturing and marketing pharmaceuticals and consumer products worldwide. Most Canadians will use at least one of its products daily. But if you asked a consumer who makes Rub A-535, they probably couldn't tell you.

Well, Carter-Horner does. It has also developed and marketed Gravol, Diovol, Ovol, Arrid Antiperspirant, Nair, Trojan Brand condoms and pregnancy kits under brand names such as Confidelle, Answer Now and First Response. In fact, Carter-Horner is among the leading over-the-counter pharmaceutical and consumer marketing companies in Canada.

More than 200 employees staff the company's manufacturing facilities in Montreal and the head office/distribution centre in Mississauga. The company's building on Kitimat Road at Argentia has been a fixture of the Streetsville area since the formation of the City of Mississauga.

Carter-Horner Inc. is a wholly owned subsidiary of Carter-Wallace Inc. of New York and reports into the company's International Division located in Princeton, New Jersey.

The company has experienced tremendous growth since the 1950s due, in large part, to its offering of innovative and quality products, well-trained sales and marketing staff and aggressive promotion. When the company introduced Arrid Extra Dry, the first antiperspirant spray, sales soared. Further growth was experienced in 1976 when Carter-Wallace Inc. purchased Denver Laboratories, acquiring Rub A-535 and Confidelle pregnancy kits in the process. Both were leaders in their respective markets.

Carter-Horner Inc. was the first company to successfully manufacture a stable, multi-vitamin liquid preparation for children, known as Infantol. That success was followed by the introduction of Gravol, an anti-nauseant that dominates the Canadian market in its category.

The addition of Trojan condoms in 1987 and First Response pregnancy kits in 1990 provided further diversification and pushed sales to record levels.

Carter-Horner has a long-standing commitment to research and development of quality products that will benefit not only Canadians, but people throughout the world. Quality and safety are paramount to the company, with products produced to the stringent standards set by Health Canada's Therapeutic Products Program.

With global trade becoming commonplace, Carter-Horner continues to aggressively pursue foreign markets and currently exports to various parts of the world, including South and Central America, the Caribbean, the Middle East and the Far East.

As a fully integrated company in Canada, Carter-Horner is constantly looking for opportunities to leverage it's substantial assets, in growing the business both in Canada and in global markets. ❖

These are only a few of the many brand names manufactured by Carter-Horner.

Bronte College of Canada

Bronte College of Canada celebrated its 10th anniversary in January 2001. Bronte College is a private, international, co-educational, boarding high school offering academic courses in Grades 9 through 12 and OAC (pre-university) levels. The college also offers English as a Second Language Programs (credit and non-credit), ESL Summer Study / Tour Camps and an Advanced Placement Program (AP).

In September 1999, Bronte College began offering a Junior and Senior Kindergarten Program (from September to June) and Grades 1 and 2 in September 2001. The Kindergarten Program is based on expectations outlined in "The Kindergarten Program" document, published by the Ontario Ministry of Education. Bronte presents a balanced program that emphasizes phonics, writing, spelling and mathematics. Instruction contains the elements of play and formal instruction in a manner that is appealing to children.

As a private institution, Bronte College offers students a great deal of flexibility in the choice of subject combinations. In addition to the basic high school curriculum, Bronte offers courses specifically geared towards those students planning to study at the university level. In celebration of its 10th anniversary, Bronte College will be expanding to include a cafeteria, library, modern computer lab and seven additional classrooms.

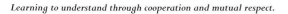

Learning to understand through cooperation and mutual respect.

Quiet residential campus conducive to learning.

To prepare international students for a university, or professionals for business purposes, Bronte College offers a comprehensive, non-credit ESL program. Students can choose to study General English, TOEFL, IELTS or Cambridge exam preparation, or a combination of these courses.

While studying in the Grade 12 level at Bronte, above-average students can participate in the AP Program. Bronte offers additional classes specially designed to help qualified students prepare for the AP exams written in May every year. Students receive a credit for each AP subject in which they successfully pass the exam. These credits are accepted by most universities in Canada and by all universities in the United States, and are treated as transfer credits in the first year of university. Students may choose the number of AP subjects they wish to write.

Bronte's unique tri-semester high school program allows students to acquire as many as 11 credits in one year. Studies run from September to December, January to April and May to July. Students may apply to enter the program at the beginning of any semester. By taking the right combination of courses, students studying at the OAC level can graduate in as few as two semesters, depending on their educational backgrounds.

Bronte College has developed an outstanding reputation for providing a learning environment that emphasizes academic excellence, individual development and self-discipline. Its highly qualified teachers are eager to help students realize their full academic potential.

Bronte College is justifiably proud that its OAC graduates have maintained a 100 per cent university acceptance rate for the past 10 years. ❖

Alcon Canada Inc.

The Alcon Story—one of almost unparalleled success and growth—began in 1945 when two pharmacists pooled their meager resources to open a small pharmacy in Fort Worth, Texas. Combining the first syllable of each man's last name, Robert D. Alexander and William C. Conner christened their fledgling enterprise the Alcon Prescription Laboratory. This modest pharmacy was the beginning of Alcon Laboratories—today a greater than $2 billion U.S. international pharmaceutical company specializing in the discovery, development, manufacture and marketing of ophthalmic pharmaceutical, surgical and vision care products. Alcon Canada represents one of the 170 markets worldwide in which Alcon operates.

Enterprising as they were, Conner and Alexander began calling on area physicians rather than wait for business to come to them. They encouraged doctors to recommend their pharmacy while simultaneously selling the vitamin preparations they had developed and asking probing questions to uncover additional opportunities for their business. The partners soon discovered that no pharmaceutical company specialized in ophthalmic products. Patients were typically instructed to take their ophthalmic prescriptions to local pharmacists, who, with varying degrees of skill and accuracy, would then prepare them using distilled water and the drugs the doctors specified. Because the distilled water was often not sterile, contamination of these ophthalmic solutions was not uncommon. Conner and Alexander then began manufacturing sterile ophthalmic products and began promoting their products to ophthalmologists.

Throughout the years, Alcon's research effort focused on developing products specifically formulated for ophthalmology. In fact, the plastic dropper bottle, now universally used for ocular preparations, was an Alcon innovation.

Alcon's leadership in the eye care market was already well established when Nestlé—an international company headquartered in Switzerland—was exploring opportunities for acquisitions in the health care field and purchased the firm in 1977. Today, Alcon is the number one ophthalmic pharmaceutical/surgical corporation in the world.

Alcon Canada Inc.'s new headquarters located at 2665 Meadowpine Boulevard, Mississauga, Ontario.

Alcon Canada Inc. was established in 1959 in Don Mills, marketing a small number of ophthalmic pharmaceuticals. Since then, Alcon Canada has grown into the number one company in Canada's eye care market. Consumers will recognize contact lens care products such as Opti-Free® Express®, anti-allergy medications such as Patanol®, along with the new LADARVision® laser for refractive surgery.

The Canadian headquarters moved to Mississauga in 1975 and now occupies a new 92,000-square-foot office/warehouse complex on 11 acres, employing 110 people on-site and more than 90 sales and after-sales service people across Canada. Alcon Canada is an ISO 9002 registered company.

Alcon Canada markets a full range of ophthalmic pharmaceuticals, surgical products, instrumentation, and contact lens care products and is the exclusive Canadian distributor for Humphrey instruments and Leica surgical microscopes. It sells its products to ophthalmologists, optometrists, opticians, ENT (Eye/Nose/Throat) specialists, Primary Care physicians, hospitals and pharmacies.

Alcon helps customers find the solutions they need to better manage the technical, clinical and business aspects of their practices. Initiatives such as the SOVA programs (Senior Ophthalmologists/Optometrists Visiting Alcon), which allow ophthalmologists and optometrists to view Alcon's research facilities in Fort Worth first hand, are part of its commitment to support continuing education and business development for Canadian eye care specialists.

Alcon Canada sponsors educational seminars in all aspects of eye care including its annual Master Club meeting, which covers a broad range of ophthalmic subjects. Alcon has undertaken an extensive clinical research program in Canada and supports a variety of ophthalmic research programs in major universities across the country. Its **Mission for Sight** emphasizes the importance of early detection and treatment of glaucoma.

Alcon Canada supports numerous Canadian medical missions through the donation of ophthalmic drugs and devices to Canadian eye care specialists who volunteer their time and skills to preserve and restore sight in developing countries. It also donates pharmaceuticals and devices to the CNIB (Canadian National Institute for the Blind) Mobile Eye Care Unit and annually sponsors the training of a Seeing Guide Dog through Canine Vision, a division of The Lions Foundation of Canada.

Through innovative products and the continued support of customers, Alcon Canada expects to reach $160 million in revenue and grow to 225 employees in the next three to five years. ❖

Hoffmann-La Roche Limited

Hoffmann-La Roche Limited, also known as Roche, is one of the world's leading health-care companies, with a global perspective on research, drug development and marketing. The year 2000 marked the company's 70th anniversary in Canada.

Roche is distinct from other pharmaceutical companies because of its ability to offer integrated health-care solutions to customers through the combined efforts of its pharmaceutical and diagnostic divisions. By bringing together the expertise of the two divisions, Roche is completely involved in screening, diagnosis, prevention, treatment and monitoring of disease. Innovations in Roche's Diagnostics Division have resulted in Nobel-prize winning Polymerase Chain Reaction (PCR) technology, which allows for genetic material to be replicated in a test tube. The company has also led major innovations in testing and monitoring for diabetes and screening for viruses. Roche has two head offices—one for its pharmaceutical division in Mississauga and one for its diagnostic division in Laval, Quebec.

Of Roche's 800 employees across the country, almost half are located in Ontario, contributing more than $38 million to the Ontario economy through income tax, corporate property tax and salaries. Of the $25 million Roche invested in research and development in 2000, approximately $12 million of that was spent in Ontario on research that included clinical trials and genetic research.

Roche makes major contributions to Ontario universities and institutions. This contribution includes academic fellowships at schools such as McMaster University and sponsorship and participation in the University of Toronto's Industrial Pharmacy Residents Program. Roche also makes contributions to many hospital research programs, including the Ottawa Heart Institute's ACES (Acute Coronary Extended Surveillance) Program—a program linking a network of Canadian hospitals involved in the treatment of heart attacks, or angina, and which collects data that can be easily accessed by doctors, nurses and researchers.

Hoffmann-La Roche Headquarters on Meadowpine Boulevard in Mississauga.

Roche also sponsors a variety of organizations, including the Canadian Breast Cancer Foundation, the Canadian Association of Emergency Physicians, the Canadian Liver Foundation, the Canadian AIDS Society and the Kidney Foundation of Canada. Roche is the largest corporate sponsor of the Heart and Stroke Scientific Research Corporation of Canada's fellowship program.

The company's current therapeutic focus includes oncology, transplant, virology and metabolism. Consumers will recognize Roche products like Xenical®, a breakthrough treatment for unhealthy weight and obesity; Tamiflu®, the first oral flu pill for the treatment of influenza; Herceptin®, the first genetic therapy for breast cancer; Xeloda®, the first oral chemotherapy agent; and Rituxan®, the first bio-tech product for non-Hodgkin's lymphoma.

In addition to product development, Roche recognizes the importance of providing patient and physician education. A recent example of this is Roche's BodyWellness Support Program. BodyWellness provides patients taking Xenical with access to a 24-hour telephone line staffed by registered nurses and dieticians with whom they can speak about nutrition and other healthy lifestyle issues.

This unique combination of pharmaceuticals and diagnostics ensures that a patient gets the right treatment at the right time. Doing this is a win for patients, a win for Roche and a win for the Canadian health-care system. ❖

Products from Hoffmann-La Roche.

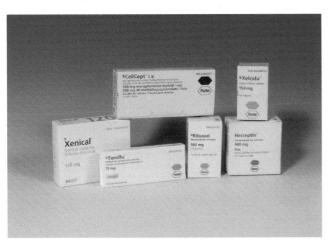

Chapter Twelve

HIGH TECHNOLOGY,
MANUFACTURING
& DISTRIBUTION

Photo by Jeff Morgan

Hershey Canada

*C*hocolate begins with a bean...a cacao bean. The scientific name for the cacao tree's fruit is 'Theobroma Cacao' which means 'food of the gods.' In fact, the Mayan Indians worshiped the cacao bean over 2,000 years ago. The history of chocolate spans from 200 B.C. to the present, encompassing many nations and peoples of our world. It wasn't until 1894, however, that Milton Hershey established what is now the most famous chocolate manufacturer in the world—the Hershey Chocolate Company.

It took Hershey another 70 years, though, to enter Canada. In 1962, Hershey Foods Corporation constructed its first plant outside of Hershey, Pennsylvania—in Smiths Falls, Ontario. Selected for its plentiful supply of milk and water, available labor source, and location on direct rail lines, the Smiths Falls facility began production in 1963 with 200,000 square feet of working space. The products introduced at the facility were 5¢ and 10¢ chocolate bars, instant chocolate, cocoa, chocolate chips and chocolate syrup. In 1965, a new production line was added to produce Reese peanut butter cups and this quickly became one of the company's best selling brands.

Hershey Canada Headquarters.

Hershey entered the non-chocolate confectionery arena in 1977 with its acquisition of Y&S Candies, one of the oldest confectionery firms in North America. The Montreal plant was opened in 1908 to produce a variety of licorice products and in 1929 the Twizzlers brand was established.

The introduction of Brown Cow, Canada's best selling chocolate syrup came in 1980, followed in 1982 by Reese's Pieces, ET's favorite snack. In 1983, the formula for chocolate manufactured in Canada was changed to a creamier and milder flavored product more suitable to Canadian taste.

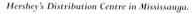

Hershey's Distribution Centre in Mississauga.

In 1987, Hershey purchased the assets and trademark rights of Nabisco Brands Ltd.'s Canadian confectionery and snack nut businesses. These businesses included candy sold under the brands Oh Henry!, Eat-More, Glosette and Lowney, hard roll candy sold as Life Savers and Breath Savers, Planter's nuts, Chipits baking chips, boxed chocolates sold under the Moirs brand name, and Care*Free and Bubble Yum gum brands. Production of the Planter's nut products and Lowney product lines were consolidated into Smiths Falls' operations. The Life Savers, Breath Savers and Planters businesses were later sold.

Moirs, one of Canada's oldest candy makers, was established in 1815, as a bakery in Halifax, Nova Scotia. Over time, the focus changed from cakes to candy and Moirs Pot of Gold boxed chocolate was introduced in 1928, now Canada's favorite brand of boxed chocolate. In 1975, production was moved across the harbor to a new facility in Dartmouth.

In 1996, Hershey Canada purchased Leaf Canada Inc., acquiring the rights to the Rainblo and Jolly Rancher ball gum, Whoppers malted candy, Jolly Rancher candy and Mr. Freeze and Jolly Rancher water-based freezer snack businesses.

From its early beginnings, through growth and acquisition, Hersheys' Canadian plants in Smiths Falls, Montreal and Dartmouth combine to produce close to 200 million pounds of chocolate, candy and cocoa-based grocery products for North American and international markets each year.

Hershey moved its Canadian headquarters to Mississauga in the early 1990s and now operates from a 40,000-square-foot complex on Matheson Boulevard East. It also leases a large distribution centre in Mississauga and has sales offices across Canada.

Aggressive, consumer-driven marketing strategies, supported by strategic sponsorships, have enabled Hershey to attain the status of the number one confectionery company in Canada. In Mississauga, it has an agreement with the city in which Hershey's name is attached to the arena (Hershey Centre)

Finishing touches are put on the construction of a "giant" chocolate bar at the entrance to the new Hershey store in Niagara Falls.

built to house the Ontario Hockey League's Mississauga Ice Dogs and serve as the city's chief sports and entertainment centre.

In 2000, Hershey sponsored the women's world hockey championships held at the Hershey Centre and presented the *Hershey Ice Classic*, a charitable fund-raising hockey game between Team Canada '76 and the Toronto Maple Leafs alumni. It also supports the annual Skate Canada competition.

Hersheys' Eat-More brand is a major sponsor of the Canadian Professional Rodeo Association and supports a pro rodeo team that travels throughout western Canada. Reese has a long-term association with Alberta Alpine, a ski-training program for potential Olympic athletes. In Ontario, the company is associated with the Southern Ontario alpine division, sponsoring a season-long racing league for the 14-to-19-year-old age group.

Also in 2000, Hershey Canada licensed the first-ever Hershey store in Niagara Falls, Ontario. The 6,000-square-foot store is at the foot of the Rainbow Bridge. It was designed in a 'contemporary retro' style, with vintage photographs and nostalgic collectibles alongside video screens and larger-than-life characters.

In the United States, founder Milton Hershey's belief that an individual is morally obligated to share the fruits of success with others has resulted in significant contributions to society. Together with his wife, Catherine, he established the most prominent of his philanthropic endeavors—the Hershey Industrial School—in 1909, now called Milton Hershey School.

Today, the 10,000-acre school houses and provides education for nearly 1,100 children whose family lives have been disrupted. Through the Hershey Trust Company, the school is a majority shareholder of Hershey Foods, and is a direct beneficiary of Hershey Foods' success.

The future of Hershey is bright, according to Rick Meyers, President and General Manager. "I continue to be impressed with the calibre of people we have been able to attract and retain. When you combine the quality of their efforts with the strength of the Hershey brands, I am confident we will continue to grow our business in Canada from our base in Mississauga."❖

Rhodia In Canada

$\mathscr{R}$hodia, one of the world's leading specialty chemicals companies, began operations January 1, 1998, as a result of the merger of Rhône-Poulenc's chemicals and fibers and polymers operations.

The roots of Rhodia, a subsidiary of Rhône-Poulenc S.A., trace back to 1858 when pharmacist Etienne Poulenc opened a small drugstore outside Paris, which later expanded to include photographic equipment, apothecary supplies and his own specialty products.

The modern history of Rhône-Poulenc began in 1895, with the creation of the Sôcieté Chimique des Usines du Rhône. The company produced a number of drugs to treat casualties of World War I and was the first French firm to produce penicillin. In 1948, the company established operations in the United States as Rhodia Inc., changing its name to Rhône-Poulenc Inc. in 1978 to identify more closely with the worldwide strength and reputation of its parent company, known as Rhône-Poulenc S.A.

By 1969 Rhône-Poulenc had become the largest company in France. In 1986, Rhône-Poulenc S.A. began to implement a program of acquisition (18 in North America), globalization and privatization. Rhodia is now a global organization, employing 26,000 people worldwide, with operating production facilities in 29 countries and sales in more than 135 countries.

Rhodia is organized into five divisions: industrial specialties, consumer specialties, fine organics, services and specialties, and polyamide. The Rhodia structure favors entrepreneurial spirit and individual initiative. Every day employees of Rhodia collaborate with customers to create innovative, ever-more high performing products in the areas of beauty, apparel, food, personal care, environmental protection, automotive and transportation that improve everyday life. Rhodia is committed to empowering teams within each enterprise, which it considers the best way to create value and promote efficient management

Product quality verification—Rhodia Engineering Plastics.

Rhodia's Canadian Headquarters, Wolfedale Road, Mississauga.

systems. Each entity is in charge of defining the tools of competitiveness for the business for which it has responsibility.

The industrial specialties division develops and manufactures high value-added products in three business lines: silicones, tire and rubber, coatings and construction materials. The division's growth is based on researching and manufacturing innovative products such as specialized silicones, highly dispersible silica, adhesion promoters and demolding agents for tire manufacturing, latex and Tolonate®. Applications of these products are found in waterproofing, detergents, automotive, apparel and textiles, paper manufacturing, house paint and construction materials.

The products and additives produced by Rhodia enhance the quality and performance of numerous end products, in areas as varied as food, cosmetics and detergents. The consumer specialties division works closely with customers to create innovative solutions, often anticipating trends in consumer habits. The division's products also are intended for specialized industries, such as metals processing, agrochemicals and petroleum development.

The fine organics division represents three fine chemicals activities: synthesizing customized molecules in its life science chemicals enterprise, and producing pharmaceutical ingredients, and diphenols and aromas for the food and fragrance markets. The division also produces intermediates—basic raw materials that are used by its businesses. The division's expertise in customized chemical procedures sets the standard for the pharmaceutical and agrochemical industries.

The services and specialties division includes three independent businesses: Eco Services, offering services to industrial enterprises for protecting the environment; Electronics and Catalysis, whose products are intended for high-tech applications; and Acetow, manufacturing acetate tow for cigarette filters.

In Canada, Rhodia employs more than 200 people and generates more than $250 million in annual revenue. Its head office is on Wolfedale Road in Mississauga.

Rhodia's engineering plastics business has selected Mississauga as the location for it its North American headquarters. Rhodia Engineering Plastics, with world headquarters in Lyon, France, is the world's second largest supplier of nylon 6 and 6.6 to the automotive, electrical and electronics and consumer goods industries. The enterprise has a sales network that spans the world, 10 manufacturing plants on 5 continents, and technical development centres in Europe, North America and Asia.

A high degree of upstream integration in its production chain gives the company a distinct competitive advantage. Rhodia Engineering Plastics' nylon products have unlimited applications because of their exceptional properties: resistance to heat and abrasion, strength, electrical properties and low flammability.

Production Line—Rhodia Engineering Plastics.

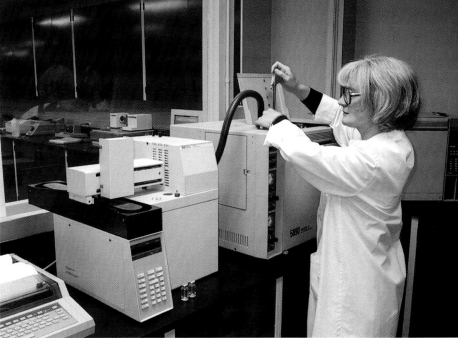

Quality Control Laboratory—Home, Personal Care & Industrial Ingredients.

The North American operations include a manufacturing facility in Mississauga and an application development centre located in Farmington Hills, Michigan, enabling Rhodia Engineering Plastics to develop new applications in partnership with its customers.

Rhodia's Mississauga facility is also a versatile worldwide manufacturer of a variety of organo-functional silicone polymers for paper and film release coatings, the mold manufacturing market, and specialty silicone release coating used for aluminum, tin or steel equipment in the commercial bakeries industry. The expert technical and industrial team research, develop and produce innovative silicone-based technologies and unique products to improve their customer's productivity levels and cost effectiveness.

The Mississauga plant also manufactures products for the consumer specialties division, which includes different types of surfactants and synthetic polymers. These products are used in a wide variety of applications such as emulsifiers, dispersants, detergents, paints, lubricants and cleaners. Other examples of the industries using these products include mining, textiles, oil field, and household and personal care products.

Rhodia is growing and succeeding by building profitable businesses that satisfy the evolving needs of its customers, challenging its employees, serving the public and establishing itself as a recognized and respected market leader. ❖

Cooksville Steel Limited

❧~❧~❧

*I*f you drive east over the Dundas Street overpass near Cawthra Road, you will see a large factory to the south. Just another multi-national spin-off so typical in Mississauga? No. This is a local success story, built by the daily effort of the Miszczuk family—residents of Mississauga for more than 50 years.

In 1928, Charles and Pauline Miszczuk left Poland, came to Toronto and began a business called Toronto Fire Escape, manufac-turing and erecting steel stairs, fire escapes and ornamental iron. They left their three sons, Chester, Ronald and Sidney, in Poland with their grandparents.

In 1939, with the threat of Germany invading Poland, Charles and Pauline had their three sons join them in Canada. In Toronto, the boys went to school and helped in their father's business. Under his guid-ance, the Miszczuk brothers learned their trade in the steel industry.

As the war progressed, Chester and Ronald enlisted in the Royal Canadian Air Force. Sidney, too young to join the forces, stayed in Toronto with his parents. The Miszczuk family business was closed due to the restrictions on the supply of steel imposed by the war.

The brothers returned safely from the war and began working for a variety of different companies.

In 1951, Chester, Ronald and Sidney started their own business, Dominion Fire Escape & Steel Works. Together they purchased one acre of land in Toronto Township, now referred to as the Cooksville area of Mississauga. Having little money, the brothers dug a foundation and poured the footings by hand and put up a small building. Adding to their struggle, all three brothers had day jobs so they worked on their building in the evenings and on weekends.

Cooksville Steel's head office in Mississauga.

The 35,000-square-foot Kitchener plant.

Once the 4,000-square-foot building was complete, Sidney was the first to quit his day job and begin the operation of their small business of manufacturing steel stairs, fire escapes, ornamental iron and 200-gallon oil storage tanks.

"We had very little money, but lots of guts," Sidney says of the enormous task.

During the late 1950s, Chester, the eldest brother, sold his share of the business to Ronald and Sidney. That was the beginning of the newly named Cooksville Steel Limited—a name that better reflected its community and would retain its heritage with the area.

In the 1960s, Cooksville Steel began fabricating, supplying and erecting structural steel for buildings. The business started to grow so they expanded. In the mid 1960s, a second branch was opened in Kitchener. The Kitchener plant grew and expanded five times to its current size of 35,000 square feet. The head office in Mississauga eventually acquired a total of approximately six acres, and the building was expanded numerous times to its current size of 45,000 square feet.

In 1978, Ronald died, leaving Sidney the sole operator of the business. In 1997, Sidney's two sons, Robert and Eric, purchased Ronald's share of the business and became active participants in the business.

"Our family made a significant contribution to the shape of what is now Mississauga," Robert Miszczuk says. "We have relationships with builders

going back to day one. We're typical
of how Canada was built—by individuals, the majority of whom were
new to Canada."

The buildings to which Robert
refers are many for which Cooksville
Steel supplied and erected the
structural steel—schools, shopping
malls, warehouses, commercial
buildings, churches, sports arenas
and factories from Northern
Ontario to the United States.

Many are very recognizable:
Waterloo University, Nissan
Canada's corporate headquarters
overlooking Highway #401 and
Johnson Controls in Ajax.

Cooksville Steel also provided
structural steel for a new mill at
the Hemlo Gold Mine in Northern
Ontario and such familiar retail
operations as the No-Frills at Mavis
and Eglinton and the Costco on The
Queensway, just east of Islington Avenue in Etobicoke.

Cooksville Steel's business investments are very diversified. Since 1980
the company has continued to be involved with Flag Resources Limited and
Golden Brian Mines Limited in the exploration of platinum, palladium, gold,
nickel and copper near Sudbury, Ontario. Flag Resources is listed on the
CDNX and Golden Briar Mines on the Montreal Stock Exchange.

The entrepreneurial spirit does not end there. Robert and Eric operate
Lakeshore Studios, a film and TV production facility located on Lakeshore
Boulevard in Toronto. Cooksville Steel originally bought the facility as an
investment in 1980. Again, the personal daily effort—the driving force of
the Miszczuk family—has turned this enterprise into an internationally
recognized part of the Toronto film business.

Cooksville maintains its core business as a prominent structural
steel fabricator in Ontario. It now employs more than 70 people between
its two plants and supplies steel for hundreds of buildings every year.

"The Mississauga we all know today is a reflection of the dedication,
commitment and investment made by Cooksville Steel and other builders,"
Sidney Miszczuk says. ❖

*Cooksville Steel supplies and erects the structural steel for buildings from
Northern Ontario to the United States.*

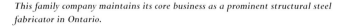

*This family company maintains its core business as a prominent structural steel
fabricator in Ontario.*

Merck Frosst Canada Ltd.

Merck Frosst Canada Ltd. is Canada's leading research-based pharmaceutical company. Though the company is based in Kirkland, Quebec, Mississauga is the base for its Ontario operations. Merck Frosst is an affiliated company of Merck & Co., Inc.

Merck Frosst discovers, develops, manufactures and markets innovative products to improve human health. The company markets an extensive line of cardiovascular products for high blood pressure, elevated cholesterol and heart failure, as well as a broad range of vaccines. Merck Frosst is also a recognized leader in the treatment of arthritis, asthma, osteoporosis, HIV/AIDS, glaucoma, prostate disease, male pattern hair loss and other diseases. The company's mission is threefold: To provide society with superior products, services and innovative solutions that improve quality of life and satisfy customer needs, to provide employees with meaningful work and advancement opportunities, and to provide investors with a superior rate of return. All of the company's actions are measured by its success in achieving this mission. Merck Frosst prides itself on delivering high quality, ethical human health products in its areas of research expertise.

Merck Frosst is responsible to customers, to employees and their families, to the environments they inhabit and to the societies it serves. In discharging its responsibilities, it does not take professional or ethical shortcuts. Merck Frosst strives to identify the most critical needs of consumers and customers and devotes its resources to meeting those needs, always adhering to the highest ethical standards.

Merck Frosst employs more than 400 scientific personnel in the research and testing of new human health products.

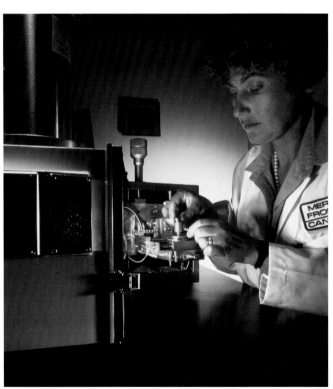

*A researcher performs **in situ** sampling of a freeze-dried product.*

The Merck Frosst Centre for Therapeutic Research is the foundation of discovery and development on which Merck Frosst continues to build its world-renowned reputation in the treatment of respiratory, inflammatory and other diseases. Not only is this recognition exemplified by the medicines that have come out of the Centre's laboratories, but also by the wealth of knowledge that its scientists have uncovered and shared throughout the scientific and technical world.

Creative spirit, dedicated effort and application of new technology form the basis for innovation that the pharmaceutical industry requires for success in today's biomedical research environment. The company positions itself at the forefront of science, utilizing novel methodologies for the improvement of human health.

Merck Frosst placed 15th among the 35 Best Companies To Work For in Canada according to a survey published in January 2001 in the Globe and Mail's *Report on Business* magazine. The company employs more than 1,700 people in Canada, including 300 of the world's leading scientific personnel. The Merck Frosst Centre for Therapeutic Research is one of the largest biomedical research facilities in Canada. The centre's mandate is to discover new therapies for the treatment of respiratory, inflammatory and other diseases. In 1999, the company invested more than $100 million in R&D in Canada.

Merck Frosst recently doubled its Ontario sales force, headquartered in Mississauga, and also operates satellite corporate offices in Toronto and Ottawa. More than 150 of the firm's employees are based in Ontario. In Mississauga, Merck Frosst has also supported the University of Toronto

A technical service specialist monitors the process parameters of the tablet-coating machine.

One of the company's key initiatives is patient health management (PHM). PHM programs are designed to cross over existing barriers in diagnosis, treatment and patient compliance to provide better health outcomes for patients, an improved quality of life and better coordination of precious health resources.

The goal of PHM is to bring providers together in a specialty area and, supported by industry expertise in that specific disease category, deliver a more outcome-based program of treatment for each patient being served. For example, a PHM program could follow a patient's compliance with their treatment program after discharge from a hospital to ensure unnecessary readmissions are avoided. Merck Frosst has already launched successful programs in Alberta, Manitoba, Quebec and Nova Scotia and is keen to expand these successful programs into Ontario in partnership with the provincial government. ❖

at Mississauga by funding the establishment of an entrance scholarship for the Masters in Biotechnology program.

Since 1997, Merck Frosst scientists have been responsible for the discovery of two major medical advances: SINGULAIR® for the treatment of asthma and VIOXX® for the treatment of pain from osteoarthritis.

Company scientists have also discovered a gene responsible for programmed cell death in the human body, a process called apoptosis. Inappropriate cell death is linked to diseases such as Alzheimer's, Parkinson's, Huntington's and certain cancers. This major scientific discovery may hold the key to discovering new treatments for these debilitating diseases.

Merck Frosst prides itself on being a knowledge-based company with heavy emphasis on human health care and health policy research and support. Through such initiatives as the sponsorship of multi-disciplinary conferences and ongoing partnerships with leading experts in academia, health policy and economics, Merck Frosst maintains an active role in the health-care community.

Merck Frosst's Mississauga office and depot.

Bridgestone/Firestone Canada

As part of an international corporation, Bridgestone/Firestone Canada Inc. (BFCA) is focused on leveraging the company's global strengths in technology and innovation to the benefit of its consumer and commercial customers. With the objective of offering products and services of superior quality, BFCA's mission is to deliver unprecedented levels of satisfaction to all its customers.

A Global Organization

Bridgestone is the world's largest manufacturer of tires and other rubber products. It manages operations worldwide through its global headquarters in Tokyo and regional headquarters in Nashville, Tenneessee, and Brussels. Bridgestone/Firestone Canada Inc. (BFCA), based in Mississauga, is a wholly owned subsidiary of the Americas organization.

Bridgestone holds more than 50 per cent of the original equipment automobile tire business in Japan and is the official supplier for more than 30 automakers worldwide. Besides making more than 8,000 different types of tires—from a 13-foot-tall giant radial for earthmoving equipment to a kart tire that stands only seven inches high—Bridgestone manufactures a wide range of industrial and chemical products and sporting goods.

The company offers a full line of tires for a variety of vehicles from passenger cars to trucks and buses to motorcycles. It also manufactures tires for subways, monorails and airplanes. Bridgestone Corporation operates 43 tire plants and 51 plants for other products in 24 countries and markets its products in more than 150 nations.

The plant in Joliette, Quebec, employs more than 1,000 people and is one of Bridgestone/Firestone's principal tire manufacturing plants.

Canadian Snapshot

Bridgestone/Firestone Canada Inc. was established in March 1990 through the amalgamation of the Canadian Bridgestone and Firestone operations. The new company moved into its current headquarters on Hurontario Street in May 1990. Bridgestone/Firestone Canada has more than 1,900 employees across Canada.

There are regional distribution centres in Moncton, Mississauga, Winnipeg and Vancouver, and a tire manufacturing plant in Joliette, Quebec. There is also a textiles facility in Woodstock, Ontario, that manufactures nylon yarns, resins and woven tire cords used in Bridgestone/Firestone products. Bridgestone/Firestone is the only tire manufacturer in the world that makes its own cords.

In Canada, BFCA distributes products through an independent network of more than 900 outlets and 45 corporately owned retail locations.

For almost a century, Firestone has been the premier tire in the world of auto racing. With over 50 wins at the Indianapolis 500, Firestone has more wins at the brickyard than all other tire manufacturers combined. Bridgestone entered Formula One competition in 1997, winning its first title just one year later.

History and Heritage

Harvey S. Firestone founded the company named after him, in Akron, Ohio, in 1900. Firestone was the first to introduce the solid rubber side-wire tire, and in 1907 introduced the first commercial demountable rim.

Shojiro Ishibashi, who transformed his small family business making tabi, traditional Japanese footwear, founded the Bridgestone Tire Co., Ltd., in 1931. He came up with the company name by reversing the English translation of his own surname: 'Ishibashi,' which literally means, 'stone-bridge' in Japanese. He preferred the

Bridgestone/Firestone Canada's head office and major distribution centre is located in Mississauga, Ontario.

sound of the name Bridgestone, very similar to Firestone, a company he greatly admired. Bridgestone entered the U.S. market in 1967 through a sales subsidiary in California.

A Leader in Technology

Bridgestone/Firestone is a leader in world tire technology. It utilizes research and development centres in Tokyo, Akron, Ohio and Rome to produce advanced tire technologies. There are world-class proving grounds in Ft. Stockton, Texas; Sao Pedro, Brazil; and Acuna, Mexico.

The UNI-T family of technologies (UNI-T, UNI-T AQ and UNI-T AQ II) is exclusive to Bridgestone/Firestone products and represents the latest in tire technology. This revolutionary system allows tires to perform well while wet, even in a worn condition. UNI-T AQ keeps performance up as the tread wears down. Bridgestone was the first tire company to introduce the 'run-flat' tire, and its Blizzak winter tire is still the standard by which all other tires are judged.

The Firestone Test Center in Columbiana, Ohio, is one-of-a-kind. It covers 350 acres of farmland and is the only facility in the world to test farm tires exclusively 24 hours a day, 7 days a week, all year. Firestone agricultural tires are tested under severe farming conditions to ensure that they outlast and outperform other farm tire brands under the most extreme conditions.

Importance of Motorsport

In 1911, to put his tires to the ultimate test and publicize their superior performance, Firestone began what would become a legendary history in car racing by entering—and winning—the first Indianapolis 500. Firestone has gone on to win more than 50 Indy 500s.

Bridgestone and Firestone products have competed in nearly every form of motorsports, including Formula 1, Championship Auto Racing Teams (CART), Indy Racing League, Monster trucks, drag racing and many more. Besides Formula 1, Bridgestone racing tires appear in series such as Formula 3000, Formula Nippon, Touring Cars and Grand Touring Cars. Bridgestone is also a force and a strong contender in karting.

In Canada, Bridgestone/Firestone Canada Inc. has been a major sponsor of both the Toronto and Vancouver FedEx CART Molson Indy events. The company also supports karting extensively, including this country's first World Championship Kart event in 2001. The company is the official tire and title-sponsor of the Bridgestone/Firestone Racing Academy at Mosport International Raceway, east of Toronto. Canadian drivers such as Jacques Villeneuve, Alex Tagliani and the late Greg Moore, all trace their roots back to this program.

Through racing, the company gains new insights and information that help Bridgestone/Firestone design and build better tires for everyday street and highway driving. ❖

UNI-T, The Ultimate Network of Intelligent Tire Technology, is a comprehensive combination of tire technologies so advanced it takes tire performance to a new level. The Bridgestone Turanza and Potenza lines of touring tires incorporate the company's new technologies, along with Bridgestone Blizzak winter tires and Firestone Firehawk performance tires.

Rockett Lumber & Building Supplies Limited

*I*f you live in a home built by Kaneff Properties, Mattamy Homes or Fernbrook Homes in Mississauga, it's likely the wood used to construct it came from Rockett Lumber and Building Supplies Limited of Mississauga.

Rockett has been supplying quality products, technical support and reliable service to the domestic and international building industry for 50 years, 30 of which have been spent in the company's main facility on Wolfedale Road, which is strategically located with access to all major highways. In 1997, Rockett purchased a yard and truss manufacturing facility in Courtice, Ontario, just east of Oshawa. In 2000, it opened a new yard in Kitchener-Waterloo to serve the needs of area builders. In the summer of 2001, Rockett again expanded geographically to Fonthill, Ontario. It purchased

certain assets of Fonthill Lumber Limited and formed a partnership with one of the previous owners. The partnership is currently operating under the name Fonthill Lumber.

In 1997, Rockett Homes International was created to supply prefabricated home packages to customers in markets worldwide. As of today, its largest markets are the United States and Ireland. It has also supplied to the Japanese and German markets.

Rockett Lumber's strong management team is able to react to the changing demand for lumber, especially when a slumping economy can result in a downturn in housing starts. The Greater Toronto Area (GTA) home construction market is the most vibrant market in Canada, if not all of North America. Rockett Lumber is a major supplier to this market and it easily anticipates and adapts to the constantly changing demands of both the domestic and international markets. It services about 7,000 new home starts annually.

The company was established in Mississauga in 1952 by Bernard F. Rockett to meet the emerging need of housing developments in the GTA. It has developed a reputation among its customers and suppliers for quality products, reliable service, sound business practices and financial stability. Through subsidiaries, Rockett Lumber has participated as in investor in new home subdivisions with major builders.

The bulk of Rockett's sales is dimensional lumber (2x4s, 2x6s and 2x8s in a variety of lengths) used in the framing of new homes. The lumber is purchased from Canadian mills in British Columbia, Ontario, Quebec and The Maritimes. Rockett also stocks Engineered Wood Products (LVL, PSL, LSL beams and Wood I-joists), plywood, insulations, hangers and all other necessary products required in the framing of a home.

All three Ontario facilities can provide accurate estimates for lumber, trusses, engineered wood products, wall panels and stairs. Professional advice on such things as building code requirements

and on-site construction is also available.

There are manufacturing facilities for roof trusses and floor trusses in both Mississauga and Courtice. Rockett Lumber also remanufactures and re-grades lumber and manufactures stairs, columns and posts at its Mississauga location.

The company's team of designers and technical sales representatives has more than 160 years combined experience in the truss industry. They provide custom design roof trusses for any building application while adhering to the design requirements of building codes in any province or state. Because they are custom engineered for every project, a wide variety of exterior profiles and ceiling shapes can be applied.

Roof trusses are delivered to the job site as pre-engineered, prefabricated systems, eliminating any on-site trimming and cutting, saving time, labor and material. Every delivery comes complete with placement layouts and engineered drawings, as well as erection and bracing information.

Each floor joist system design is custom engineered and is structurally superior to conventional systems. A professional engineer checks every Rockett-engineered floor system. Both open wood-webbed and metal-webbed systems are available, allowing for open basements and the elimination of dropped ceilings. A Rockett floor system is easier to handle and lighter than conventional lumber and because full joist lengths are used, there are fewer pieces to connect and installation time is reduced.

Rockett's team of designer engineers is trained on CAD and automated wall assembly. Wall panels provide a precise, consistent finished product every time. Installation is easy, and all walls link together to form a snug, precise fit.

The company's stair manufacturing division, opened in 1994, has developed into one of Ontario's major stair suppliers. The company has 50 skilled craftsmen with combined experience of more than 250 years in the manufacturing and installation of stairs. All stairs are custom handcrafted from Canadian hardwoods and softwoods. Circular, straight and winder varieties are available.

Rockett Lumber plays a dynamic role in community and business organizations. It sponsors amateur sports teams and raises funds for organizations such as the Knights of Columbus and the United Way. The company has been an active participant in the Lumber and Building Materials Association since 1961, the Greater Toronto Homebuilders Association since 1966 and the Mississauga Board of Trade since 1982.

The company's success has been built on reacting to changing customer and industry needs. With a dedicated, experienced staff, an outstanding product lineup and 50 years of success to fall back on, Rockett Lumber is well positioned to retain its market position in the new millennium. ❖

VWR Canlab

VWR Canlab's customers know this company well. They know it as a company whose continued growth and success is a direct result of its strong customer focus. The combination of philosophy, geography, systems, product, people and special services gives customers a feeling that they have received more than they expected.

Test tubes, ovens, fridges and just about anything else you would find in a lab are available from VWR Canlab. The company's customers come from the biotechnology sector, universities, pharmaceutical companies, hospitals, mining companies and food and beverage firms.

Its Canadian headquarters is located in an attractive, but unassuming building on Argentia Road, just west of Erin Mills Parkway.

It is the biggest company in its sector in Canada and has more than 200 employees Canada-wide, about 110 of whom work in Mississauga—including the sales staff. There is also another facility in Montreal and a warehouse in Edmonton.

The VWR Canlab dedication to quality is apparent from a customer's first encounter with the well-trained associates. They make sure they clearly understand a customer's requirements and have the expertise to help clients decide which products will most completely and cost-effectively meet their needs.

To guarantee satisfaction, VWR maintains the largest inventory of laboratory supplies and equipment, thus ensuring orders are filled and shipped within 24 hours. If a product isn't in stock, virtual warehousing allows sales

The state-of-the-art Radio Frequency Scanners used in VWR Canlab warehouses improve accuracy and give the company the ability to trace orders and operations "real time."

representatives to order directly from the inventories of key suppliers. VWR has access to about 400,000 products worldwide and deals regularly with more than 2,000 vendors.

VWR provides a series of systems-related products and services designed to streamline and assist the ordering process. The company attempts to make sure its products and services are more than satisfactory to customers by applying Total Quality principles. The result is lower costs, better turnaround on orders, the highest fill rate in the industry and an accuracy rate of 99.8 per cent.

"The real value of our continuous and consistent approach toward meeting our customers' requirements means that they can concentrate on their core business: making science happen," says Alison Murphy, vice-president and general manager for Canada.

"Our mission is to distribute the highest quality products and provide systems solutions and services that create the maximum value for customers, employees and suppliers," Murphy says. The formula, obviously, is working to perfection.❖

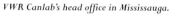

VWR Canlab's head office in Mississauga.

Subaru Canada, Inc.

Subaru automobiles are one of the best-kept secrets in Canada—except to those who drive them.

Subaru Canada, Inc., headquartered in Mississauga, is dedicated to offering Canadian drivers vehicles that are built to exceed customer expectations. Subaru believes in the wisdom of preventing accidents before they happen. That's why every Subaru comes with All-Wheel Drive (AWD), developed over the past 25 years by a dedicated group of people who understand the need for safety.

Building a better, more reliable vehicle that challenges existing measures of performance, durability and safety is what Subaru does best. The company's Canadian network of 100 dealers coast-to-coast offers professional advice and service. Mississauga is the central clearing house for all parts nationwide.

Legacy GT Sedan. What grand touring is meant to be. The much acclaimed Subaru Legacy. Proof that beauty can be more than skin deep.

Subaru has a proven track record for its performance on the world rally stage, where the Impreza WRX has taken the company to three consecutive World Rally Championships for manufacturers. Subaru uses the knowledge it gains from building winning rally cars to engineer cars that have high levels of active and passive safety for the average consumer.

Most people are likely to think of Subaru as a small company; in fact, it is a part of one of the world's largest conglomerates—Fuji Heavy Industries Ltd. (FHI) of Japan, a leader in many areas of transportation. Besides the automotive division, FHI has an aerospace division backed by 80 years of aircraft manufacturing experience, as well as a transportation division that builds railcars, and an ecology systems division that builds refuse collection, separation systems and dissolution systems.

The bus manufacturing division develops and manufactures bus bodies, and the house fabricating division develops unit-assembled, prefabricated minihouses.

The industrial products division has developed high-performance, high-quality engines that are used for everything from construction to leisure craft.

However, it is in the automotive sector that Subaru really shines.

The Outback was the first All-Wheel Drive vehicle to bridge the gap between sport-utility capabilities and car-like comfort—perfect for Canadian drivers. The Forester also offers the toughness Canadians expect in their sport utility vehicles while providing car-like comfort. Its low centre of gravity, driving performance and outstanding cargo-carrying capacity make it perfect for driving to and from work or for a rugged, safe drive to the cottage or ski hill.

The Impreza is rally-tough, but available with power windows, locks and mirrors, fog lights, a rear spoiler and alloy wheels—all the little touches Canadians demand. The Legacy is available in either wagon or sedan layout and is perfect for big families or small. The influential Insurance Institute for Highway Safety in the U.S. has named Legacy and Forester safest in their respective categories.

While performance, safety and durability are important to Subaru engineers, they have not forgotten about the environment. They are continually working to reduce engine emissions while increasing fuel efficiency on every Subaru. At the same time, they are developing more and more components that can be recycled.

Subaru has no rivals. It truly provides solutions for the road ahead. ❖

The WRX Experience. Defying the laws of physics. Impreza for 2002. Versatile, sporty, rugged, sizzling.

Band World

Tony Bennett, Crosby Stills Nash & Young, The Barenaked Ladies, Leslie Cheung, Andre Phillipe Gagnon, Shania Twain, Ricky Martin, James Brown, Faith Hill, Neil Sedaka, Loretta Lynn, Destiny's Child, Ray Charles, Paul Anka, Julio Iglesias, Wynonna Judd, the Beach Boys and Kenny Rogers—despite the differences in their music, all have one thing in common—they have worked with Band World, of Mississauga at one time or another.

Bob Spencer, Band World's president, is a former bandleader and touring artist who continues to produce variety shows and concerts worldwide. Band World was incorporated in 1988 and is now a major force in both the entertainment and corporate industries. Clients include the Canadian National Railway, Fidelity Investments, Molson Indyfest, Mirvish Productions, the City of Toronto, the City of Oakville, the City of Mississauga, Casino Rama, Casino Niagara and the Chinese Cultural Centre of Greater Toronto.

Band World is involved in the production of the Brazilian Ball, the Cathay Ball, the Teddy Bear Affair, Reach for the Rainbow's Crystal Ball, Molson Indyfest, Waterfront Festivals for Oakville, Belleville, and Mississauga, the Watershed Festival for Walkerton, Canadian Music Week, and the City of Toronto Winterfest and Street Festivals.

Band World is a full-service production company. It is located close to all major highways and its facilities are within easy reach of numerous major suppliers and manufacturers. This provides the company with an extensive network of sources for equipment, materials and supplies, an important factor in Band World's ongoing commitment to providing the highest quality service available.

Canadian National "CN—The Railroad of Tomorrow—The Timeless Railroad of Today" 2001 Allie Award for Best Themed Entertainment.

Band World uses state-of-the-art audio speaker systems. It is one of only two Canadian companies licensed to own the V-Dosc system, a revolutionary wavefront sculpture technology that allows for optimum coverage. Canadian Music Week has awarded Band World the 'Concert Support Service Company of the Year' award for the past two years and the 'Best New Technology for Live Touring' award. Band World's expert audio technicians have pleased clients and their audiences in the SkyDome, Air Canada Centre, Maple Leaf Gardens, the Metro Toronto Convention Centre and the Mississauga Living Arts Centre.

Band World maintains an extensive inventory of lighting fixtures, computerized lighting, rigging and ground support systems. Its award-winning lighting staff can provide full-size concert lighting, or portable lighting for smaller events.

Band World provides customers with any format and size they require for a presentation, incorporating both audiovisual and multimedia elements to make the event come alive for the audience. This service can include computer graphics, Power Point presentations, custom slide shows, pre-recorded sound tracks and live video projection.

Room decor adds the ultimate finishing touch to any corporate event. Band World will help design and integrate a decor theme and can provide customers with all the elements to make an event sizzle.

Band World delivers the highest level of service possible, which, combined with creativity, imagination and skilled professionals ensures total satisfaction for its clients. ❖

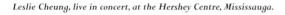

Leslie Cheung, live in concert, at the Hershey Centre, Mississauga.

Photo by Michael Scholz

Chapter Thirteen

TRANSPORTATION
& ENERGY

Photo by Michael Scholz

Enersource Corporation

It has a new name, a new logo and a new boss, but Hydro Mississauga is still providing Mississauga residents and businesses with safe, efficient and reliable electricity service 84 years after it started.

The new company is Enersource Hydro Mississauga and it's led by industry veteran Gunars Ceksters, president and chief executive officer of the parent Enersource Corporation. The same efficient utility that froze residential electricity rates for seven consecutive years, Enersource Hydro Mississauga continues to maintain rates that are among the lowest in Ontario. It is the company with the best safety record in the history of the Canadian electricity distribution industry and several successive record-breaking years of system reliability.

Deregulation, mandated by the Ontario government in 1998, is changing the role of the electricity utility in many ways. Around the world, deregulation is designed to enhance competition and bring consumers more choice. For businesses, it means working within a new and challenging environment. In the case of Enersource Corporation, separate affiliate companies will allow it to promote commerce and return dividends to the tax-paying citizens of the City of Mississauga.

The corporation is 90 per cent owned by the City of Mississauga and 10 per cent owned by Borealis Energy Corp., a subsidiary of the Ontario Municipal Employees Retirement System (OMERS).

Enersource Corporation was established to separate Enersource Hydro Mississauga into businesses that are subject to regulated rates of return and those that are not. The name "Enersource" was chosen for its simplicity and effectiveness in encompassing the expanding range of energy products

Mississauga resident Ramil Pineda and his young family can take advantage of competitive rates and group buying power offered by the corporation's new associated retail energy company "First Source."

Enersource Hydro Mississauga employees, including Dave Raven towering here over the Mississauga landscape, continue to set new safety records in the Canadian electricity utility industry.

delivered, and the historical role of the municipal utility as a trusted community-based energy source for consumers.

While Enersource Hydro Mississauga is the regulated "wires" part of this business that will continue to deliver electricity reliably and safely to its customers' doors, unregulated Enersource Corporation businesses currently include Enersource Technologies, a businesses that specializes in providing expertise in engineering and construction; Enersource Telecom, specializing in fibre-optic cable connections throughout Mississauga; and Enersource Hydro Mississauga Services under its new "First Source" brand that offers retail energy effective at the opening of the market.

Employees are key to any company's success and many great people have played significant roles in building Enersource Hydro Mississauga to its current status as one of the premier electricity utilities in Ontario. In order to maintain their leading-edge expertise, its employees keep up with the latest developments, improving their knowledge of highly advanced technologies.

Enersource is also offering new choices for its customers, such as new bill payment options including "e-bill," allowing customers to use the Internet to receive and view their account statement and make payments online.

Early in 2001, Enersource Telecom announced a multi-million dollar undertaking to develop a fibre-optic infrastructure in the City of Mississauga. Using its right of ways and existing poles and conduits, the company began engineering and constructing a fibre-optic support system stretching more than 100 kilometers across the city. Ultimately, it hopes to become Mississauga's "last mile" provider, making high-speed broadband connections to any point within the city's service area.

Enersource Technologies, specializing in engineering, procurement and commissioning, builds upon the core strengths of its employees to provide competitive business-to-business services such as substation maintenance, substation engineering, sub-metering and energy reporting, UPS systems and backup generation. One project the company is currently involved with is the massive reconstruction of Pearson International Airport, the busiest airport in Canada and among the Top 30 in the world.

Throughout all of these non-regulated businesses, and perhaps more in the future, Enersource is exploring projects, products and services that cut across traditional utility boundaries. Change for this company means creating tangible business opportunities.

Enersource Corporation—proud to be "Your Community Connection." ❖

Lineman Paul Tremblay and Vaffi Poonja, General Manager of Enersource Technologies, discuss electrical plans for the redevelopment of Pearson International Airport.

Students at Meadowvale Secondary school are among those who will benefit from the new high-speed access that Enersource Telecom will be providing to every school in the Peel Region.

In addition, the content-rich enersource.com Web site offers an online tool for customers to report when lights are out in their neighborhood and request cable locates before digging.

In order to maintain its record of reliability, Enersource continues to invest in excess of $3 million annually in the cyclical replacement of buried electrical cables. The company has in excess of 10,000 kilometers of distribution circuits and 44,000 street lights, which it maintains on behalf of the city.

Using its expertise, Enersource has launched a number of new initiatives and formed separate affiliate companies that offer a wide range of competitive products and services Among these new businesses are Enersource Telecom, Enersource Technologies, and "First Source."

Enersource Corporation has joined forces with other Ontario utilities and under the "First Source" name is optimizing group-buying power in order to offer competitively priced services to its customers.

In the deregulated market, electricity is traded on the stock market as a commodity and prices can go up and down hourly. "First Source" offers firm contracts in order to limit the customers' exposure to spot market price fluctuations and allow them to better control their operating expenses.

Petro-Canada

❧

*P*etro-Canada is a major oil and gas company and a leader in the highly competitive Canadian petroleum industry. Like the many amateur athletes and Olympic hopefuls it supports, Petro-Canada understands what it takes to compete against the best in Canada and around the world: focus, discipline and the capability to achieve results.

To ensure future success and superior business results, Petro-Canada is strategically focused on four core businesses: East Coast Offshore, Natural Gas, Oil Sands and the Downstream. Complementing Petro-Canada's business plan is a strong commitment to invest in Canada's future through a number of innovative and unique programs.

East Coast Offshore

With interests in every major Grand Banks discovery to date and newly acquired prospects in the Flemish Pass Basin and Scotian Shelf, Petro-Canada is a major player off Canada's East Coast. Strong production growth is expected in the next few years as Petro-Canada holds a 20 percent interest in the producing Hibernia oil field, the first Grand Banks development and is the operator and majority interest owner of Terra Nova, the next Grand Banks oil development. Unlike Hibernia, which produces oil from a concrete platform, Terra Nova oil will be pumped from the seabed into a vessel capable of processing 140,000 barrels a day.

Natural Gas

Petro-Canada is one of the largest producers of natural gas in Western Canada, with daily production in excess of 700 million cubic feet. For long-term growth, Petro-Canada continues to strategically explore and develop potential in the Alberta Foothills, northeastern British Columbia and west-central and southeastern Alberta. The company is also evaluating the future

Petro-Canada is the largest producer of lubricant base stocks in Canada and one of the largest producers of pharmaceutical and food-grade white oils in the world. Photo by Albert Normandin

To ensure future success Petro-Canada is focused on four core businesses: East Coast Offshore, Natural Gas, Oil Sands and the Downstream.

natural gas potential of the Mackenzie Delta region in the Northwest Territories and off-shore Nova Scotia. Petro-Canada is positioning itself for future northern exploration and development in Alaska with the acquisition of exploration rights to about 323,000 acres on the North Slope. The company is encouraged by geology very similar to the Alberta and British Columbia foothills.

Oil Sands

Petro-Canada is a leading participant in the development of northern Alberta's vast oil sands resources. It has a 12 percent working interest in Syncrude, the world's largest oil sands mining operation and significant interests in areas where bitumen can be extracted *in situ* (in place), such as the 30,000-barrel-a-day MacKay River oil sands project. The company will use steam-assisted gravity drainage (SAGD) technology to extract the bitumen with less surface disruption than traditional mining operations.

Downstream

In the Downstream, Petro-Canada transports, refines, distributes and markets crude oil into a full range of petroleum products and related goods and services. The Downstream head office is located in Mississauga in Sheridan Park and is home to close to 400 employees.

• *Refining*

Petro-Canada owns and operates refineries in Edmonton, Montreal and Oakville. These facilities produce a full range of refined petroleum products, including gasolines, diesel oils, heating oils, aviation fuels, heavy fuel oils, asphalts and feedstocks for lubricants and petrochemicals. The company is committed to continually striving to improve the reliability and environmental performance of its operations.

With its clean gasoline blend, SuperClean, together with WinterGas and other products targeting Canada's unique driving conditions, Petro-Canada is Canada's Gas Station.

• *Marketing*

Petro-Canada is Canada's Gas Station, the only Canadian-controlled company with a national retail and wholesale network. It currently markets the second-largest volume of petroleum products in Canada, including retail sales to motorists and home heating, farm, industrial and commercial customers. The company operates a retail and wholesale network of nearly 2,000 sites across Canada. Its clean gasoline blend, SuperClean, together with WinterGas and other products targeting Canada's unique driving conditions, continue to position Petro-Canada as the brand of choice for Canadians. Petro-Points, the company's branded customer loyalty program continues to expand with a membership that includes close to 5 million households.

• *Lubricants*

Petro-Canada is the largest producer of lubricant base stocks in Canada and one of the largest producers of pharmaceutical and food-grade white oils in the world. Its state-of-the-art lubricants facility at Mississauga utilizes a two-stage hydrotreating process that is unique in Canada. This process enables the company to refine gas oils produced from a wide range of crude feedstocks into lubricating oil base stocks with the highest level of purity of any base stocks in Canada. Petro-Canada lubricants are produced at the Mississauga plant and in demand around the world.

Investing in Canada's Future

Petro-Canada's success as an energy company depends on the support of Canadians. The company is determined to earn that support, not just through excellence in meeting customer needs, but also by playing a significant role in Canadian life.

Petro-Canada is working to achieve its social vision by focusing on the development of Canadian talent, innovation and expertise through education. The company invests in a wide range of educational programs for young people, including several environmental initiatives. It supports many non-profit organizations that deliver much-needed health and social services to Canadian communities.

As well, Petro-Canada is an enthusiastic supporter of Canada's amateur athletes and Olympic dreams through its investment in the Canadian Olympic Association and the Petro-Canada Olympic Torch Scholarship Fund. The fund, designed to encourage young Canadians to balance their pursuit of athletic excellence with their educational goals, was created as a lasting legacy of the cross-country torch relay leading up to the 1988 Calgary Winter Olympics. Since then, scholarships valued at more than $5 million have been awarded to more than 1,700 athletes and 150 coaches.

By focusing on its core businesses, exercising discipline in achieving objectives, ensuring the company has the financial and organizational capability to carry out its plans and investing in Canada's future, Petro-Canada will further increase its ability to successfully compete against the best in the world. ❖

With interests in every major Grand Banks discovery to date and newly acquired prospects in the Flemish Pass Basin and Scotian Shelf, Petro-Canada is a major player off Canada's East Coast.

Transpro Freight Systems Ltd.

Don't ask Frank Prosia or Joe Carusi, co-owners of TransPro Freight Systems Inc. of Mississauga, to move one of the company's tractor-trailers—neither man has ever drove a truck, or even rode as far as five miles in one.

But that's about the only thing the two don't know about the trucking business.

TransPro was founded in 1989 and incorporated in 1990 just as North America was heading into a deep recession. Prosia, a 1981 Sheridan College graduate, had worked at TNT Overland Express, first as a sales and marketing co-ordinator at the Mississauga office, and moving up to a management position by 1987. Carusi, a Ryerson grad, came aboard to provide an organizational structure to support sales.

Deregulation of the trucking industry was opening up new ways of offering shippers superior service and cost savings. Reduced demand forced companies to cut inventories and switch to just-in-time production and delivery. TransPro identified a need and acted quickly to the change.

One of the many trailers depicting Athletes in Action used by Transpro to promote the City of Toronto's Bid for the Olympic Games.

"The recession was the best thing that ever happened to us," Prosia admits. "Businesses were forced to find more efficient methods of moving their goods along the supply chain." Our current location (on Columbus Road) is our fourth location. We've gone from a small humble beginning of 3,000 square feet, then 10,000 and now a state-of-the-art, 25,000-square-foot cross-dock trucking terminal. At times during this process, we had to tell our sales staff to stop selling because we just couldn't keep up with the escalating growth."

The partners believe that the trucking industry is basically a people industry and is essentially technology proof; you'll always need a truck. "To us, trucking is a service, not a commodity," Carusi says. "People are our biggest asset—along with being located in Mississauga."

"Mississauga is the transportation hub of Ontario and Canada," Prosia adds. "All the major 400 series highways dissect Mississauga and the airport is close as well. Besides, Joe and I were both raised in Mississauga and continue to have our family roots here so it was a natural fit."

Trucks need highways to operate efficiently and effectively and because Mississauga is the centre of the Canadian trucking industry, there is a large resident labor force, highly skilled to meet TransPro's needs.

TransPro offers an exclusive Direct Driver Service. The same truck carries the customers' load from origin to destination on less than truck-load shipments. TransPro was one of the first companies to offer satellite tracking in 1994, and its dedication to service led the company to become one of the first trucking companies to become ISO 9002 certified. The firm's continuous learning program has enabled staff to be highly trained and collectively one of the best teams in the industry.

"We don't pretend to do it all. We have perfected our service as a transborder trucking firm, and we work hard to be the best at it. A true testament to our company's strength has been the fact that our customers from the early days are still with us, and we have grown together."

That's why TransPro has twice been named one of Canada's Top 100 fastest growing companies and was named Small Business of the Year in 1998 by the Mississauga Board of Trade.

Prosia, Carusi and TransPro are all big Mississauga boosters. TransPro is involved with little league hockey and soccer and sponsors a number of activities. Prosia was a member of the United Way of Peel golf tournament organizing committee, helping raise more than $100,000 every year he was on the board, and assisting the Rotary Club of Mississauga with their Fund Raising Auction.

When mayor Hazel McCallion called on local companies to support the City's involvement in the Toronto bid for the 2008 Olympics, TransPro Freight responded by advertising the spirit of the games for the Toronto Bid Committee on eight trailers.

"Joe and I are truckers at heart, without the AZ licenses," Prosia says. We've become truckers with a corporate look. We bring professionalism to our industry and promote our employees to do the same. Trucking is the most important link in the distribution channel.

"Until a customer has his goods delivered damaged free and on time, a shipper's sale is not possible. We intend to grow our fleet at a manageable pace without jeopardizing the service our customers have come to expect. Slow steady growth eliminates growing pains, allows for better trained staff, a clearer vision and will help us achieve the long-term goals of the company."

TransPro customers include Revlon Canada, General Electric, Bayer Corp., Magna International and Xerox Canada.

Ask any TransPro customer the one thing they can say about the service they receive and it's unanimous: "We can sleep at night knowing that TransPro will deliver."❖

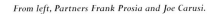

From left, Partners Frank Prosia and Joe Carusi.

Testcor

Most Mississauga residents likely don't give a thought to how Hydro Mississauga determines how much electricity they use. They probably know there's a meter somewhere outside their home but have no idea how it works or who designed and manufactured it. The bill arrives and they pay it.

If only it were that simple.

Who makes sure every meter is measuring correctly?

Meters are complex pieces of equipment and must be calibrated to within strict tolerances dictated by Measurement Canada. With deregulation of the electrical supply business, more and more companies are competing for business. In order to certify a meter, these companies are required to be government accredited and to have approved meter test equipment. Olameter Inc., for example, has set up business in Mississauga and has six of Testcor's meter test consoles in operation.

The cost of a new console is approximately the same as the price of a small home in Mississauga. It takes about four months to design, build and test before it's delivered to the customer.

Testcor is one of the largest meter test equipment manufacturers in Canada and is currently seeking ISO 9001:2000 certification.

Testcor is also working on a new test console design that will have two powerful new test modes and include real time diagnostics and test analysis. It is being designed to higher levels of safety and accuracy than currently available in the industry.

"The new console will be solid state, hands free and automated," David Lloyd president of Testcor says, "We're hoping to cut the construction phase in half." Lloyd and the employees at Testcor are dedicated to producing a quality product, and it is apparent that this is truly the kind of business where patience is a virtue. Release is expected in the fall of 2001.

Testcor Inc. specializes in the design, manufacture and servicing of meter test equipment and software.

Performing daily accuracy checks and meter verification with Testcor built equipment at Olameter Inc.

Lloyd designs and builds both the console and the software used to operate it. He studied electrical engineering technology and then worked with similar equipment for Consumer and Corporate Affairs Canada (now Measurement Canada). His career path continued on to Etobicoke Hydro and J. K. Johnstone Meters Limited where he merged his company Comptrol Instruments Ltd. From there, the concept of Testcor Inc. became reality.

All test consoles built at Testcor's Mississauga Trader's Boulevard Facility are calibrated and tested for compliance to Measurement Canada's specifications then shipped to the customer's location. Here government inspectors retest the console for an approval that can span up to three years before retesting is required.

Lloyd selected Mississauga as the home of Testcor "because it's appealing from a business perspective. It's booming, and it seemed like a good place to locate a small business. It has strong leadership and a vibrant hydroelectric commission."

Currently, more than 25 Testcor consoles are located at utilities across the country. Lloyd's goal now is to penetrate the lucrative U.S. market. "The U.S. certainly provides excellent growth opportunities for our firm," Lloyd says.

It's likely that if you live or work in Mississauga, your hydro electricity meter is tested using Testcor equipment. ❖

Federal Express Canada Ltd.

Federal Express Corporation was founded by Frederick W. Smith, chairman and president. In 1965, as a Yale undergraduate, Smith wrote a term paper about the passenger route systems used by most airfreight shippers, which he viewed as economically inadequate. Smith stated that what was needed was a system designed specifically for airfreight that could accommodate time-sensitive shipments such as medicines, computer parts and electronics.

In August 1971, after a stint in the military, Smith bought controlling interest in Arkansas Aviation Sales, located in Little Rock, Arkansas. While operating his new firm, Smith identified the tremendous difficulty in getting packages and other airfreight delivered within a day or two. This problem motivated him to do the necessary research for resolving the inefficient distribution system. Thus, the idea for Federal Express was conceived.

The company, incorporated in June 1971, officially began operations on April 17, 1973, with the launch of 14 small aircraft from Memphis International Airport. On that night, Federal Express delivered 186 packages to 25 U.S. cities—from Rochester, New York to Miami, Florida. Today, FedEx is the largest express transportation company in the world and is the second largest airline, in terms of number of aircraft, in the world.

The Canadian headquarters, on Explorer Drive in Mississauga, plays a key role in the FedEx system. Federal Express Corporation purchased its six-year-old Canadian licensee, Cansica Inc. and began operating as Federal Express Canada Ltd. in 1987.

FedEx was the first Canadian courier to use dedicated airlift. Today, FedEx utilizes a Canadian domestic air network that includes four Boeing-727s and additional feeder airlift, providing next-day coast-to-coast service.

FedEx aircraft, which comprise the world's largest all-cargo fleet, have a combined lift capacity of more than 26.5 million pounds daily. In a 24-hour period, FedEx planes travel nearly one-half million miles.

Today, FedEx Express handles about 3.3 million packages and documents every night.

The new Canadian corporate headquarters, opened in the summer of 1999, consolidated employees from three different locations in the Greater Toronto Area. FedEx now has more than 5,000 employees in Canada. The 62 stations link Canada to more than 210 countries worldwide.

FedEx Canada is very community minded. For example, it supports Junior Achievement of Peel by providing financial assistance, discounted shipping and staff volunteers who talk to the students about exports, customs and technology.

The FedEx corporate philosophy—People-Service-Profit (P-S-P)—has three corporate goals that form the basis for all business decisions.

The *people* priority acknowledges the importance of employee satisfaction and empowerment to create an environment where employees feel secure enough to take risks and become innovative in pursuing quality, service and customer satisfaction.

Service refers to the consistent and clearly stated service quality goal of 100 per cent customer satisfaction, 100 per cent of the time.

The *profit* aspect is the end result of the first two principles. If People provide Service, Profit will result.

FedEx's Leadership Evaluation Awareness Program (LEAP) is a process implemented to improve leadership effectiveness and retention. LEAP is compulsory for any employee who wants to progress to management level positions within the company.

Today, FedEx handles about 3.3 million packages and documents every night. FedEx aircraft, which comprise the world's largest all-cargo fleet, have a combined lift capacity of more than 26.5 million pounds daily. In a 24-hour period, FedEx planes travel nearly one-half million miles. FedEx couriers log 2.5 million miles a day, the equivalent of 100 trips around the earth. ❖

Ontario Power Generation

Ontario Power Generation (OPG) is helping to build a bright future for Mississauga and Ontario. A successor to Ontario Hydro, OPG is a new company with a history of service and commitment going back to the early 1900s.

OPG is a major, Ontario-based producer of electricity owning 3 nuclear generating stations, 6 fossil-fuelled stations and 69 hydroelectric stations. OPG's revenues for the year 2000 were $5.9 billion with a net income of $605 million.

OPG's fossil-fuelled Lakeview Generating Station in Mississauga plays an important role in meeting Ontario's and the area's power needs, especially during the summer when air conditioning use increases. Fossil-fuelled generation is essential to Ontario because of its ability to respond quickly to customer electricity needs during times of high demand. In 2000, Mississauga's electricity use accounted for five per cent of that consumed in Ontario—while the city's summer demand has recently grown at an average of 4.4 per cent a year, double the summer peak demand growth of the province.

In recent years, about 25 per cent of OPG's electricity has come from its fossil-fuelled stations, which are amongst the cleanest and most competitive fossil-fuelled generating facilities in North America.

OPG has made significant investments in its Lakeview and other fossil-fuelled stations to enhance their reliability, lower costs and reduce air emissions. Since the early 1980s, the company has invested more than $1.8 billion in new clean-air technologies at its fossil-fueled stations, including scrubbers, low-nitrogen-oxide burners, the purchase of premium low-sulphur coal and the greater use of natural gas. Today, OPG's fossil-fuelled stations are producing more electricity than they did in the early 1980s but with almost 60 per cent lower acid-gas emissions, enabling the company to continue to meet Ontario's growing energy needs in an environmentally responsible way.

The remainder of OPG's generation comes from its hydroelectric and nuclear generating stations. Over the past five years, these facilities have generated more than 75 per cent of OPG's electricity and are both cost effective and have virtually no emissions contributing to smog, acid gas or global warming.

In addition to meeting customers' needs for clean, reliable electrical power, OPG is an important employer and economic contributor. The company directly employs 12,000 people throughout the province—including more than 600 employees and their families living in Mississauga. In 1999, OPG also purchased $220 million of goods and services from more than 100 large and small Mississauga businesses. This includes more than $2 million of purchases by the Lakeview Generating Station.

OPG strongly believes in enhancing the quality of life in communities where its plants operate.

From January 1999 to December 2000, the company contributed about $1.5 million to over 200 education initiatives across the province. This included funding to the Gordon Graydon Memorial Secondary School in Mississauga who entered an OPG-sponsored team in the Canada FIRST Robotic Games that were held in Hamilton in 2000 and again in Toronto in 2001.

OPG and its employees have also worked alongside the community to support many worthwhile community-based initiatives—including the Rotary Club of Mississauga, Port Credit's Carassauga Festival, the Interim Place Women's Shelter, the Lakeview Business Association's Sunset Concert Series and the Mississauga Amateur Radio Club emergency network.

Electricity is essential to the growth of Ontario's economy and the development of its communities. OPG will continue to provide customers with a reliable and competitively priced supply of this vital commodity and do so in a safe and environmentally responsible manner. ❖

Lakeview Generating Station.

Photo by Eric Berndt

Enterprise Index

The Office People Business Centres
165 Dundas Street West, Suite 900
Mississauga
Phone: 905-306-1464
Fax: 905-306-2820
Page 102

Ontario Power Generation
700 University Avenue
Toronto, Ontario M5G 1X6
Phone: 416-592-2555
www.opg.com
Page 154

Orlando Corporation
6205 Airport Road
Mississauga, Ontario
Phone: 905-677-5480
Fax: 905-677-2824
E-mail: garrigand@orlandocorp.com
www.orlandocorp.com
Pages 96-97

Pallett Valo, LLP
90 Burnhamthorpe Road West, Suite 1600
Mississauga, Ontario L5B 3C3
Phone: 905-273-3300
Fax: 905-273-6920
E-mail: mgottheil@palletvalo.com
www.palletvalo.com
Page 101

Petro-Canada
2489 North Sheridan Way
Mississauga, Ontario L5K 1A8
Phone: 905-804-4500
E-mail: custsvs@petro-canada.ca
www.petro-canada.ca
Pages 148-149

Rhodia In Canada
3265 Wolfedale Road
Mississauga, Ontario L5C 1V8
Phone: 905-270-5534
Fax: 905-270-4737
E-mail: lesley.russell@us.rhodia.com
Pages 130-131

**Rockett Lumber &
Building Supplies Limited**
3350 Wolfedale Road
Mississauga, Ontario L5C 1W4
Phone: 905-275-1800
Fax: 905-279-7984
E-mail: aldo_bartolini@rockettlumber.com
www.rockettlumber.com
Pages 138-139

Rogers Cable Inc.
3573 Wolfedale Road
Mississauga, Ontario L5C 3T6
Phone: 905-273-8000
Fax: 905-273-9661
www.rogers.com
Pages 108-109

Sheridan College
1430 Trafalgar Road
Oakville, Ontario L6H 2L1
Phone: 905-845-9430
Fax: 905-815-4081
E-mail: infosheridan@sheridanc.on.ca
www.sheridanc.on.ca
Pages 116-117

The Shopping Channel
59 Ambassador Drive
Mississauga, Ontario L5T 2P9
Phone: 905-565-3500
Fax: 905-565-2641
E-mail: customerservice@TheShoppingChannel.com
www.TheShoppingChannel.com
Page 110

Subaru Canada, Inc.
5990 Falbourne Street
Mississauga, Ontario L5R 3S7
Phone: 905-568-4959
Fax: 905-568-8087
E-mail: egriffin@subaru.ca
www.subaru.ca
Page 141

Testcor
125 Traders Boulevard East, Unit 2
Mississauga, Ontario L4Z 2H3
Phone: 905-501-1888
Fax: 905-501-0226
E-mail: corporate@testcor.com
www.testcor.com
Page 152

Transcontinental Printing
1 Place Ville Marie, Suite 3315
Montreal, Quebec H3B 3N2
Phone: 514-954-4000
www.transcontinental-gtc.com
Page 111

Transpro Freight Systems Ltd.
6855 Columbus Road
Mississauga, Ontario LST 2G9
Phone: 905-795-9494
Fax: 905-795-9477
E-mail: frankp@transpro.on.ca
www.transprofreight.com
Pages 150-151

**Turner & Porter
Funeral Directors Limited**
2180 Hurontario Street
Mississauga, Ontario L5B 1M8
Phone: 905-279-7663
Fax: 905-279-2470
E-mail: peelchapel@turnerporter.ca
www.turnerporter.ca
Page 105

University of Toronto at Mississauga
3359 Mississauga Road
Room 3134, South Building
Mississauga, Ontario L5M 1X1
Phone: 905-569-4656
Fax: 905-828-5474
E-mail: mwells@credit.erin.utoronto.ca
Pages 114-115

VWR Canlab
2360 Argentia Road
Mississauga, Ontario L5N 5Z7
Phone: 800-932-5000
Fax: 800-668-6348
E-mail: canada_callcentre@vwr.com
www.vwrcanlab.com
Page 140

Index

᪡᪡᪡